60 Choic

in the

CHILTERNS

for YOU! Beginner to Experienced

Typical Chiltern's tranquil scene

Written by Dick Chapman

7. Lower Cadsden

8. Cholesbury

5. Stokenchurch

1. Hambleden

2. Pishill

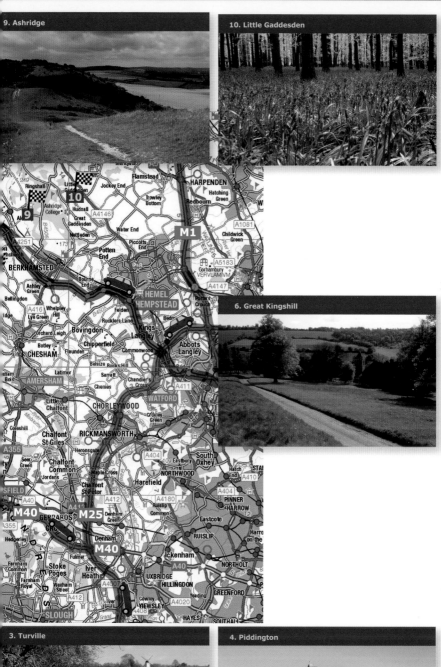

9. Ashridge

10. Little Gaddesden

6. Great Kingshill

3. Turville

4. Piddington

Acknowledgements

I am very grateful to my Chilterns walking group for their assistance in checking all the walks, being careful to remember to do so 'through the eyes of the inexperienced map reader' and constructively criticising the contents of this Guide in all aspects. I am also grateful to the owner of the 'the face' for allowing me to photograph his hedge for the front cover.

As walkers, we are all indebted to the Chiltern Society for their organisation of some 200 volunteers to help Councils maintain footpaths and other rights of way in the Chilterns. The Chiltern Society volunteers clear paths, repair and install new stiles/ gates, set up waymark posts to indicate correct path lines and, where appropriate, paint white arrows on the trees (very comforting to follow these, when walking longer distances through the many beech woodlands). It means that the Chilterns are a very accessible area for the general public to walk in.

Once you have become addicted to exploring this tranquil area, you may want to become a member of the society.

Tel:01494 771250 or email office@chilternsociety.org.uk

© Dick Chapman
First Edition 2018
ISBN 978-1-9999588-0-0
Printed in UK.
A catalogue record for this book is available from the British Library.

The author, publisher and copyright owners cannot take responsibility for loss or injury to persons or property as a result of following the routes and advice given in this Guide.

Whilst every effort has been made to achieve accuracy of information, the countryside changes over time. Stiles become gates, permissive paths may disappear, paths that are easily managed in fine weather can change to become muddy and slippery in wet weather.

If you find an inaccuracy in the maps or text, please email Choice Walks Ltd at the address below and, if it could be useful for current readers of the Guide, it will be posted on our website.

This edition published in 2018 in Great Britain by Choice Walks Ltd.
www.choicewalks.co.uk • info@choicewalks.co.uk

Table of Contents

10 Locations each with 6 choices of graded walks between 2-13 miles:

Introduction

My aim in writing this guide is to tempt the general public, especially families living within an hour's drive (which includes the whole of West London), to come and explore this wonderful area of tranquillity; the ideal place to escape to.

I say 'especially families' because it is they who have the most to gain. Children have space to let off excess energy across open fields and beech woodlands; they delight in climbing trees and seeing the wildlife e.g. Red Kites (see photo opposite), deer, pheasants, squirrels, rabbits and also the farmers livestock e.g. cattle, horses, sheep, pigs; it's a huge adventure for kids. The family dog is given a treat... all those new smells! As for mum and dad... well, first of all they'll feel good because of their commitment to having fit and healthy children; then they'll love the country pubs, windmills, thatched cottages, ancient churches, wild flower meadows and fantastic hilltop views, being such a contrast to urban living. The Chilterns are not only beautiful to behold, but are an oasis of peace and calm; tranquillity is the trade mark of the Chilterns. The contrast between that and the rush and bustle of urban life is a very pleasant surprise that awaits anyone stepping out onto Chiltern footpaths for the first time- enough to encourage them to want to repeat that surprise time and time again.

So why aren't the footpaths swarming with escaping urbanites at the moment? Because most guidebooks are written to suit experienced walkers. They don't cater for people who are inexperienced at map reading; such people not only fear getting lost in the myriad of paths that link all the villages in the Chilterns, they don't feel they own the necessary walking gear for the whole family e.g. boots, rucksacks, maps. This guide has been specially written for families to go on short, starter or 'taster' walks, in normal clothing and trainers or wellies, with the necessary maps included in this guide; everything you need to get started. All **you** have to do is believe in that day's fine weather forecast and jump into the car; but don't forget your brolly (just in case). However, **beware**- you can quickly become addicted to exploring the Chilterns and be adding walking gear to your Christmas present wish-list so that you can plan to visit the Chilterns in all weathers and at any time of the year. You can even design a weekend break, or a week's holiday based on this guide.

What's that? I can't stop you getting lost? Well, no, but I have built into the system a number of features that help you avoid getting lost (including teaching the essentials of map reading), plus a way to quickly get you back on track should you (despite all my best efforts) chatter your way past a turning you should have taken!

It is also important, from a family point of view that you know where you can park, where you can get refreshments and that you have a choice of walks from a single location. Why the latter? Flexibility. For example, you may have done the 'taster' short walk before lunch and

Red Kite

then, having had a good lunch in the pub, want to go for a longer walk as the sun is still shining and you hadn't got lost in the morning! Matters are catered for by having six choices of walk at each of the 10 different locations; walks range in distance from 2 -13 miles. Each location has parking and refreshment facilities available- allowing you to decide whether to picnic or to treat yourselves to a lovely country pub snack/ meal.

So which location do you choose? All 10 locations are in what I call the heart of the Chilterns; that lovely area (part of the Chilterns Area of Outstanding Natural Beauty) between the Thames and the Dunstable Downs. So it depends whether you are going to whizz to tranquillity along the M4 (Southern Chilterns), the M40 (Mid-Chilterns) or the M1 (Northern Chilterns). The locations map on pages 2 and 3 will help you decide.

Dick Chapman

p.s. This guide is for YOU! For the beginner, to enjoy becoming experienced; for the experienced to enjoy not only the 60 fully described walk choices, but also (possibly) 42 other walk choices, too. See page 96.

Introduction

Your first decision is which location you want to start at and whether you are going to want to take a picnic or take refreshments on site. Directions as to where to park if picnicking are given on the front page of the location (including the post code of the pub for your Sat Nav). If you are taking refreshments on site, it shows consideration to phone the pub to let them know you're parking your car in their car park, and that you'll be in for lunch (or whatever). The decision about location may be easy for you- start with the nearest to home! But you may be interested in visiting a 'special interest' place as well as going for a walk; so a look through the special interest page of the location may be productive.

Following the section for the inexperienced map reader, I explain the Sat Nav equivalent system I use for getting you back on track, should you go wrong. This system should enable you to relax and enjoy a walk, even if it's the first countryside walk you've ever been on.

Finally, I explain how you can use Geocaching (treasure hunting) to give added encouragement to your kids to come with you on an adventure.

*Note: the guide has been designed so that the **description** of a walk is on the **same** or **facing page** as its **large-scale map extract,** so that when you open the book you always see the **two together.** For ease of following a route, it is worth investing a few pounds in a **standard map case** into which the book fits neatly, open-paged. Hung round the neck, the description and the route are then easy to see in all weathers.*

Experienced map reader

If you are an experienced map reader you'll probably just look at the routes and simply follow the map extracts in the Guide (i.e. ignoring the directions). There is something extra that you'll probably make use of, too. It'll be the link every km (about every 15 minutes walking time) between the checkpoint shown on the map and the equivalently numbered paragraph in the description. Why will you need that? Because distractions happen; a Red Kite flies over; you're chatting; whatever. Suddenly, you've missed a turning and looking at the map doesn't match what you're looking at ahead. A short back-tracking, linking the description to the map, will put you quickly back on the right track. *See page 96 for 42 extra walk choices for the experienced map reader.*

For the techies

1. There are many areas of the Chilterns where there is no mobile phone signal.
2. GPX files can be downloaded from www.choicewalks.co.uk

Inexperienced map reader

There are a number of things you need to know before you set off:

1. Why can't you just follow the directions and ignore the map?
2. We are in England. Why the metric?
3. How does knowing the distance represented on the map help you?
4. You need to understand a certain number of basics about map-reading.
5. You need to recognise this Guide book's symbols.
6. You need to understand the rules I apply in giving directions.
7. Your first attempt at map reading can be in theory (can't get lost there!!)

1. Why you can't just follow the directions and ignore the map.
Because the map gives a pictorial representation of where you are, and your actual location on the map can be checked every 15 minutes walking time (see Sat Nav equivalent system, below)- which helps tremendously should you go wrong for any reason.

2. Why the metric?
Put simply, because the Ordnance Survey (OS) maps are made up on the metric scale, it's easier to learn distances on maps in metric.

If you look at the inside cover, you will see that on shorter distances i.e. within visible range, there is no noticeable difference between yards and metres and so it doesn't really make any difference if you measure in yards. For longer distance decisions, such as the length of the walk you're thinking of taking, you'll see that the mileage is shown first (with the kilometre equivalent in brackets);being in England, we think in miles!

3. How knowing the distances represented on the map help you on the ground:
One of the main ways of preventing you going wrong is for you to frequently check your location against the map. The possibility to do so is made by the positioning of checkpoints (red and white numbered octagonal shaped symbols) along the route **every kilometre**. The description of the walk which you will be following has paragraph numbers within red and white octagonal shapes corresponding to those on the map i.e. showing where you are on the map. It takes approximately 15 minutes to walk a kilometre (you will learn from practice to adjust the timing to your own speed of walking) so you can clearly see where you should be every kilometre on the map. Also on reading the subsequent numbered paragraph, it is easier for you to judge how long it is going to take you to reach any turning you have to make within that next 15 minutes.

4. Basic 'need to knows' about map reading.
You need to be able to recognise, and understand the meaning of, symbols used on the maps (extracts of the main symbols below are taken from inside back cover 'Key to map symbols'):

a) Public rights of way and other access

- ------------ Footpath
- — — — — Bridleway
- ᛭ ᛭ ᛭ ᛭ ᛭ Byway open to all traffic
- ᛬ ᛬ ᛬ ᛬ ᛬ Restricted byway (not for use by mechanically propelled vehicles)

- ◆ ◆ ◆ Long distance route / National Trail
- ------------ Permissive footpath
- — — — — Permissive bridleway

b) Waymarks/signs

The Ridgeway and the Icknield Way are ancient long distance trails. The South Bucks Way, and The Chiltern Way are examples of longer distance (more local) routes. Our routes sometimes join and leave them under direction.

c) Heights

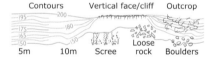

The contour lines give a pictorial representation of changes of height. On our routes, you only meet the 5metre, not 10 metre interval representation, with the actual difference in height between the lines being 5 metres (just over 16 feet); the wider they are apart on the map, the flatter the landscape is. So if your route **crosses** very closely shown contour lines, then you are ascending, or descending a very steep hill. Where your path is shown to run in **parallel** with contour lines, you are walking on the level (perhaps along a valley floor).

d) Use of inverted commas Where in a description a name of a wood (for example) is in inverted commas, it means that you can see that name on the map extract to give you extra confidence of your location. If the name of a road, or house name, (for example) is shown without inverted commas it means you will see it on your walk.

e) Terminology. The words 'metalled road' are used for describing a track, drive or country road that has a level, stony, surface of tarmac, grit or concrete, when you might have expected just hardened earth.

5. This Guide book symbols

1 Checkpoint number (also walk directions paragraph numbers)

Viewpoint

➡ Direction of walk

—— Short walk

—— Medium walk

—— Longer walk

6. The rules applied to giving directions.

I considered it very important to have the directions and the map to which they relate on the same or facing page as much as possible, for ease of linking the two together. No details of special interests (e.g. churches, manor houses etc) are given in the text, rather references to them are given separately. Footpaths are always signed public rights of way(there is a waysign/ white arrow on a tree etc); no mention is normally made of whether you have to go through gates or over stiles as it will be obvious to you, on your walk.

7. Try map reading in theory, by 'finger walking'.

Visit the section ' For the inexperienced map reader' immediately following, and linked to, the Hambleden Short walk

Sat Nav equivalent system

A car's Sat Nav system enables you to travel in a relaxed manner on a new journey, possibly via unknown roads, villages and towns to your pre-selected, possibly never visited before, destination. I want you to 'travel' on your first walk with me in that same relaxed manner, even if you've never map-read before. The steps you need to take are the following:

1. Having chosen your walk, parked your car and are ready to set off, turn to the page of your walk. If that walk is either a short walk, or a medium walk, the written description will be either on the same page as the map extract, or on its facing page i.e. you don't have to turn a page to link the written instructions to the map. You will see that the number 1 paragraph is pictorially represented on the map in the same symbol at the start of the walk.

2. Each paragraph describes the decisions you have to take in the next (approximately) 1 km i.e. approximately 15 minutes walking time. Any decisions you have to make, such as '**turn left**', are shown in **bold**. With practice, you'll be able to look at the map to see just what you're going to meet on the path in the next fifteen minutes e.g. am I going to have to go up a hill? Am I going to go through a wood? How long is it going to take me to the first decision point?

3. After a kilometre you should arrive at the next checkpoint, which will normally be a turn of some kind, and recognise exactly where you are on the map. You will be re-assured that you have not gone wrong!

4. You then repeat that process for the next and subsequent kilometres, being re-assured every 15 minutes or so that you haven't gone wrong and so arrive safely back at your starting point (being a circular walk).

5. But what if you don't recognise where you are? For example, you continue walking for longer than you expected and come to a road that is not mentioned in the directions! Help! This is where the equivalent of the Sat Nav system comes into play. You must have been chatting away, or been distracted in some way; you've not turned left (or right) at some point along the way when you should have done. In my car, the Sat Nav system lady says very politely 'make a 'u-turn' as soon as possible'. This is your equivalent. You need to turn round, and re-trace your steps until you recognise where you went wrong or arrive back at the previous checkpoint and set off again determined to concentrate! You won't be lost and you will have recovered your position quickly.

Geocaching (treasure hunting for all ages)

I say 'all ages' because of the number of families or groups of young adults I've seen walking in the Chilterns countryside, whilst at the same time enjoying Geocaching. I'm not going to describe the details of Geocaching here, so if you're interested, look it up on the internet. Like the countryside itself, it doesn't cost you anything in itself to take up, apart from the need for a mobile phone app or a GPS. The following may help you when using this book in relation to Geocaching:

1. Overall, build in a search for Geocaches along the route of any one of the walks, by using the checkpoint grid references given on the location front pages.

2. As an example: if the Hambleden Medium is the walk you've chosen to do, check if there are any Geocaches reasonably close to the route:

a) Go to the Geocache website and search for Geocaches using the post code of the Stag and Huntsman pub given on the location page for Hambleden.

b) In Hambleden Medium's case, there are 6 caches close by (at the time of going to press) that could be built in to the Medium Walk (near Checkpoint 2 'A Hambleden Bonus'; near Checkpoint 4 'GMS A16'; near Checkpoint 6 'GMS A15'; near Checkpoint 7 'GMS A17'; near Checkpoint 8 both 'Spark's Valley Spot' and 'Hambleden Hickey Hole')

c) The number of caches and closeness to checkpoints will vary tremendously from location to location, but it is amazing how this worldwide phenomenon has caught on. Caches are all over the place!

Other Matters

IN GENERAL
Follow the country code:
1. **Be safe- plan ahead and follow any signs.**
2. **Leave gates as you find them.**
3. **Protect plants and animals and take your litter home..**
4. **Keep dogs under close control.**
5. **Consider other people.**

1. Walking on country roads without pavements.

There are a few short stretches of country roads that need to be walked along as part of some of our routes. Keep on the right hand side of the road (so facing on-coming traffic) until you come to a right hand bend., when you should cross over and then return after the bend.

2. Walking near livestock- do's and don'ts.

Do stop, listen and look on entering a field. Look out for any animals and if there are any, make sure your dog is on a short lead. Normally everything will be peaceful and tranquil and you should go through the field without any problem, possibly having to divert off the path to go around a herd, but never walking between a cow and her calf (cows can be very protective of their offspring). Sometimes cattle can become interested, and follow you. Don't panic, or run, just walk on quietly and they'll lose interest.

Don't hold on to your dog if it disturbs cattle- let it go as the cattle will chase the dog and not you.

Do find another way round the field if cattle are blocking the path, or being aggressive (for example, in the pheasant season –October to the end of January- cattle can be frightened by nearby gun fire).

3. Clothing and footwear.

Choose the clothing and footwear suitable to both the distance planned and the weather conditions. For example, on short 'starter' walks in dry, warm weather, trainers and jeans are fine. But in wet, muddy conditions on a winter's day, you should wear strong walking boots or shoes that give a good grip; and wear warm, waterproof clothing.

4. Food and drink.

Take sufficient snacks and water - you can quickly dehydrate.

Tourist Information
For information regarding accommodation of all kinds (Camping, Youth Hostels, B & B, Hotels) visit the Chilterns AONB (Area of Outstanding Natural Beauty) website, where there is an interactive map providing the latest information:
www.chilternsaonb.org or the Tourist Information Centres listed:

Abingdon 01235 522711
Aylesbury 01280 823020
Berkhamsted 01438 737333
Dunstable 01582 891420
Hemel Hempstead 01442 234222
Henley on Thames 01491 578034
High Wycombe 01296 382415
Maidenhead 01628 796502
Marlow 01628 483597
Newbury 01635 30267
Oxford 01865 686430
Princes Risborough 01296 382415
Thame 01844 212833
Tring 01442 823347
Wallingford 01491 826972
Wendover 01296 345643
Windsor 01753 743900

1. Hambleden

Start point: The Stag and Huntsman, Hambleden Village, Henley-on-Thames, Oxfordshire RG9 6RP 01491 628400. Parking in public car park beyond the inn.

Hambleden's picturesque village is in the heart of the Hambleden Valley, with its surrounding hills and ancient hilltop settlements. It is the perfect place from which to explore both the valley and the hills- which we do!

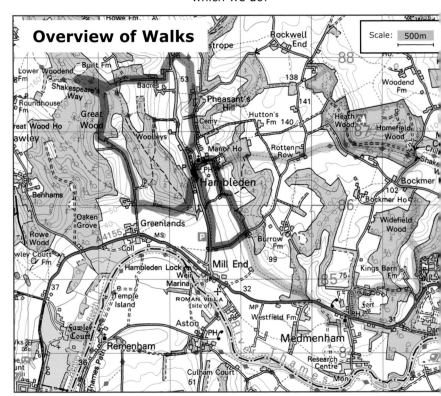

Walk Choices	Circular Walks	Distance	Ascent	Allow
	Short	**2 miles**	**25m**	**1 hr**
		3.2km	80ft	
	Medium	**4½ miles**	**120m**	**2 hrs**
		7.2km	390ft	
	Longer	**7 miles**	**100m**	**3½ hrs**
		11.2km	330ft	
	Figure of eight walks			
	Short + Medium	**6½ miles**	**145m**	**3 hrs**
		10.4km	470ft	
	Short + Longer	**9 miles**	**125m**	**4½ hrs**
		14.4km	410ft	
	Medium + Longer	**11½ miles**	**220m**	**5½ hrs**
		18.4km	720ft	

Special Interests	S	M	L	Local (Miles)
Outstanding viewpoints	✓	✓	✓	
Beech woodland		✓	✓	
Hambleden Church 12th century cruciform church.	✓	✓	✓	
Manor House Elizabethan Manor House opposite church.	✓	✓	✓	
Homefield Wood Nature Reserve with wild flower Meadow including rare orchids			✓	
Medmenham Camp Iron Age Hill Fort			✓	
Hambleden Lock Long weir to cross Thames				1
Chiltern Valley Winery and Brewery Tours and tastings				1½
Next nearest pub: The Frog at Skirmett, RG9 6TG, 01491 633996				2
Nearest towns:				
Henley-on-Thames				3
Marlow				3½

Checkpoint grid references for GPS /Geocaching (Treasure Hunting)

Short
1	SU786 865
2	786 853
3	787 862

Medium
1	SU786 865
2	781 859
3	775 860
4	770 868
5	767 877
6	774 877
7	778 878
8	782 878

Longer
1	SU786 865	**8**	815 847
2	791 866	**9**	807 848
3	800 866	**10**	804 844
4	805 870	**11**	800 847
5	815 866	**12**	792 851
6	815 861	**13**	790 854
7	816 855	**14**	789 861

Hambleden Village

HAMBLEDEN SHORT WALK

2 miles (3.2km) • Ascent 25m (80ft) • Allow 1 hour.

A gentle 'taster' walk with very little ascent, yet with unimaginably fine views across the Thames and Hambleden Valleys.

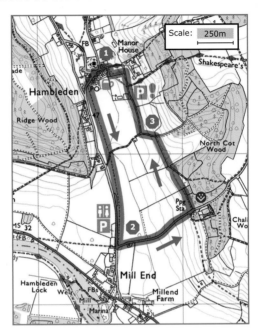

Checkpoints:

(1) Come out of the car park, **turn left**, and pass the Stag and Huntsman pub and the Church and **proceed in the direction** of the main road. **Cross** a small bridge (the riverbed is mostly dry) and **turn left** into a field. Proceed **straight ahead** over two fields for 1km (nearly ¾ mile) aiming towards the distant hills that lie on the other side of the Thames. Along the way, you have good views particularly to your left. When you reach the top right hand corner of the second field, **turn left** onto a narrow lane signposted to Rotten Row.

(2) **Proceed** up the lane for 550m (over ¼ mile) aiming for the point where the wood meets the field to your left; you have had to ascend some 25m along the lane to that point. **Turn left** onto a footpath that runs along the foot of 'North Cot Wood'. As you enter the field from the lane, you are greeted with a fantastic panoramic view that holds as you **proceed ahead**, with the wood on your right. **Cross** several fields to come off the path onto a track and **turn left**.

(3) **Descend** on the track for 75m and **turn right** onto another track that leads you back to your starting point.

FOR THE INEXPERIENCED MAP READER
a 'finger' walk on Hambleden Short route

I assume, in this section, that (by using this book) this is the first time you are going to combine a description with a map to achieve a successful pre-routed circular walk in the countryside. By leading you (now) with a 'finger walk' along the **Hambleden short walk**, I'm going to cover the **six main difficulties** inexperienced map readers normally have in tackling such a Chilterns' walk:

1. Knowing which footpath to take.
2. Judging the distance on the map.
3. Recognizing where you are on the map.
4. Putting a timing on distances between decision points (e.g. turnings left or right and checkpoints).
5. Understanding how the landscape is represented on a map.
6. Knowing how to get back on track if you go wrong.

Finger walk along the Hambleden Short walk
(refer to the map and description on the opposite page)

Note: that the **numbers** superimposed **on the map** (1, 2 and 3) are also the cross-checkpoint **numbers** of the **descriptive paragraphs** on the page opposite.

A. Number 1 is the starting location. On the map extract, **as pictorial representation**, you can see a blue pint mug representing the pub; a blue 'P' representing the car park and a tiny black square with a cross above it representing the church *(Note: the key to symbols is on the inside back cover of this guide)*.

B. **Paragraph 1.** 2nd sentence. ... '**and turn left into a field.**' There will be a signpost there to guide you. You are told to '**walk across two fields for 1 kilometre**'. You can see how far that is on the map (to the Checkpoint 2 point) but how long will that take you to get there? The walking speed for the 'average' family is about 4km per hour. So one km is about 15 minutes.

C. **Paragraph 1** 4th sentence '**good views to your left**'. You can see on the map that you are somewhere along the path towards checkpoint 2, so looking to your left (when you do the walk) the landscape changes from flat field to hills. This is represented on the map by the brown contour lines, which are 5 metres in height difference between each line. So the closer the lines are together, the steeper the ascent/descent. The '**good views**' therefore, refer to the green, pleasant (and tranquil) hills you'll be looking at on the walk.

D. **Paragraph 2 (checkpoint 2 on the map)** is where you turn left out of the field onto the lane, signposted Rotten Row. This is a very quiet road and you have to 'proceed up the lane for **550m**'. How far does **550m** look like **on the map** in comparison with the **1km (1,000m)** length of walk down the two fields? **About half....** So expect it to take you 7-8 minutes to walk the

550 metres to the turn off.

E.   There is a '**Viewpoint**' superimposed on your map extract as you enter the field. You'll enjoy the view! ❧

F.   **Notice on the map, too,** the name of the wood on your right 'North Cot Wood'- which is included in the description to give you extra reassurance that you are on the correct path (there's a wood!)

Now you should be able to continue to link the description to the map and return safely to your car.

If you follow that procedure, of **checking your position on the description** with **that on the map every km** (the checkpoints being approximately 1 km apart - 15 walking minutes), you shouldn't go wrong on a walk. But if you **do miss a turning** because of chatting or the footpath sign is covered with foliage or whatever, **you'll know** because **you may walk longer than 15 minutes** and **not recognise where you are. Simply backtrack for a few minutes until you spot what you were looking for.**

....

Hambleden Lock. Under '**special interest**' for Hambleden location is shown '**Hambleden Lock**'. You can see exactly where the lock is on the map **(bottom left!)** You could plan to visit it **as a diversion at Checkpoint 2** (you can **now judge that the distance** on the map as being approximately **10 minutes walking time** from Checkpoint 2); or you can re-park your car at the other car park after your walk (shown with a blue symbol close to Checkpoint 2 on the map) and stroll down from there. **Well worth a visit, however you do it.**

Hambleden Lock 1 mile from Hambleden

Hambleden Bear

Hambleden Valley

Marlins Grove

HAMBLEDEN MEDIUM WALK

4½ miles (7.2km) • Ascent 120m (390ft) • Allow 2 hours.

A very varied walk, with up-hills and down-hills and in and out of woodlands before strolling back for the last km along the Hambleden Valley floor; great views on the way.

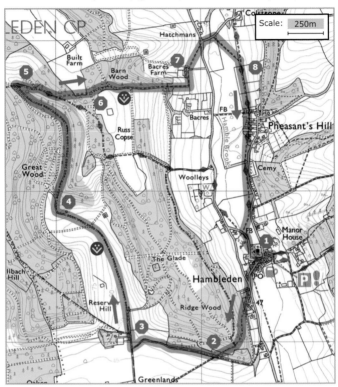

Checkpoints:

1 Come out of the car park, and **turn left**, passing the Stag and Huntsman pub, the Church and **proceeding ahead** to the main road. **Cross over** onto a path and **ascend** steadily through woodland to then **descend** ahead, on the same line, to a bridleway on the edge of the woods.

2 **Turn right** on the bridleway for 550m (over ¼ mile), with views between trees and bushes over the Thames Valley, before **turning right** at a 'T' junction of bridleways.

3 **Keep ahead** on the bridleway, which becomes metalled, with wide views of fields and woodland. **Ignore left and right** turnings for a kilometre (over half a mile) as you enjoy views all round… particularly, turning right around to look across the Thames Valley, as the path rises to enter 'Great Wood'.

4 The bridleway continues in 'Great Wood' for another kilometre, levelling out after a while, before reaching a multiple crossing point.

5 **Turn sharp right** to come off the metalled track (bridleway) and climb steadily **bearing right** on a wide track. There are white arrows on trees to guide you. *Note: This is a good place to look at the angle of the path on the map.* **Take care,** after approximately 250m, to **turn left off the track** onto a narrow footpath **winding upwards** into the woods. **Follow the white arrows** on the trees for approximately 200m to come out onto a wide multi track crossing and **proceed straight ahead.** A white arrow on a tree in front of you guides you onto the right path.

6 You now **enter** 'Barn Wood' on a wide, metalled track that goes quite steeply downhill for nearly 600m, with fine views to the left as you descend, to turn left round 'Bacres Farm'.

7 As the track turns right in front of the farmhouse, come off the track **ahead** onto a footpath that crosses a field half right for 175m to a road. **Cross the road** to proceed down Colstrope Lane for 75m before **turning right** onto a footpath. The footpath goes **half right** across two fields. On the second field, there is no visible path, so aim for the top right hand corner and go through a gate to **turn right.**

8 **Keep ahead** on this path for just over a kilometre as it crosses a field, goes between gardens, and then crosses two more fields. All along there are fine views to the right. In the last field, the path slopes to the right to come to a road. **Turn left,** then go through the Hambleden churchyard and return to your starting point.

Inside Hambleden Parish Church

HAMBLEDEN LONGER WALK

7 miles (11.2km) • Ascent 100m (330ft) • Allow 3½ hours.

A lovely walk where you start off climbing steeply to turn around and admire views across and down the Hambleden Valley and includes visiting a wild flower meadow and passing through an Iron Age hill fort; includes great views over The Thames Valley, too.

Checkpoints:

1 **Turn left** out the **back of the car park** directed by the Chiltern Way / public footpath signposts. **Cross** the field and **turn right** onto a track. 100m on, **turn left** onto a footpath (the Chiltern Way) up a steep hill which demands a pause now and again to turn and admire the view both across, and down, the valley. **Enter** a wood, for a short period, before coming out onto a field at the top of the hill.

2 **Go ahead** across three fields, with wide, distant views, to come to a lane. **Turn left** and stay on the lane for 150m until it bends left at Rotten Row.

3 **Come off** the lane onto a footpath directly ahead (still on the Chiltern Way) and proceed straight across the field, passing through another gate in the centre and then, aiming slightly to the right (there is no visible path), arrive at a lane. **Turn right** on the lane for 125m, then **turn left** onto a narrow, twisting path that takes you down through woodland ('Heath Wood') to the floor of the valley.

4 **Turn right** onto a wide track on the valley floor and stay on it for over 1 km (over ½ mile) until you reach a lane. Note: just before reaching the lane, on the left, is the Homefield Wood Nature Reserve, which includes a wild flower meadow.

5 **Turn right** on the lane and climb steadily for 400 m (¼ of a mile), coming to a 'T' junction and **turn left** onto another lane. **Go ahead** for just 150m and **turn right** (immediately after the houses) into a field.

6 **Cross** the short field, heading to the left of electricity pylons, crossing a stile, a driveway and **entering** a wood (Marlin's Grove). **Follow the white arrows** on the trees as you wind down, then up, then down again, with a wide field to your left, before coming out of the wood to cross the valley floor.

7 The path turns right after passing through a gate on the other side of the valley and winds up a short way before levelling out. It now runs for 800m (almost half a mile) just inside the wood, with a wide field to the right and great views both forward and to the right of the valley. **Keep ahead** until the path meets a drive, on which you **turn right**. *Check on the map: you are very close to the main road.*

8 The driveway (metalled) winds left then passes houses to continue as a footpath going around the outside of a house's perimeter fence. At its front drive, **turn right.** Go past The Old School on your right and shortly afterwards **turn left** onto a footpath opposite the front door of The Old Laundry.

9 **Cross** a drive and, just 50m beyond it, **turn right** into a wood, site of Medmenham Iron Age Hill Fort. Keep going ahead following arrows, and **descend** to a road. **Turn left** to immediately cross a main road ahead and go down Ferry Lane. **Turn right** onto a footpath after 75m.

10 **Proceed ahead** through a wooded area to cross a field keeping to the right hand edge. Then cross an old metalled track (old road) to go through a gate and **turn right** onto a permissive path. The path keeps to the right hand edge of a field, curving round left at

the end of the field, with high trees separating it from the main road, which the path shortly joins.

11 **Turn left** on the main road (good roadside footpath) for 75m, **cross** the road and **ascend** on the footpath opposite. Good views are to the right. After 75m **fork left** and go ahead on the level through a wood. **Come out** of the wood into open fields, with a wonderful panorama in front and over the Thames valley to the left. After 250m, cross a track and keep ahead with the path sweeping round slightly to the right at the same level. There is no visible path, but look ahead, aiming for a **white post.**

12 **Cross a track** at the post and continue ahead to cross two stiles into an open field and **continue straight across.** You can see Hambleden church ahead and there are good views to your left. No visible footpath, but the exit onto a road is where the hedge coming up from the left meets the woodland to your right.

13 **Turn right** on the road and then immediately **left** onto the continuation of the path, along the edge of 'North Cot Wood'. Cross several fields to come off the path onto a track and **turn left.**

14 **Descend** on the track for 75m, then **turn right** on another track to come back to the starting point.

2. Pishill

Start point: The Crown Inn, Pishill, Henley-on-Thames, Oxfordshire RG9 6HH 01491 638364. Customer parking at the inn.
Non-customer parking at Pishill church
(just down the road from the pub.)

Pishill lies in the most tranquil, beautiful area of the Chilterns. Whilst overall perhaps the toughest walking of the ten locations, it is also possibly the most rewarding, including visiting the stunning grounds of Stonor Park and the many outstanding viewpoints.

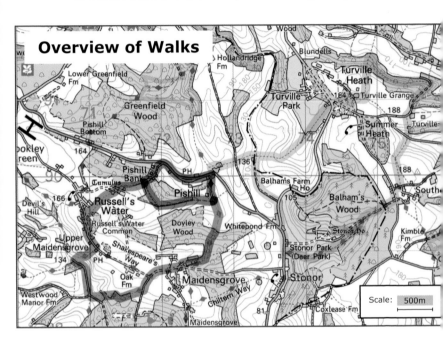

	Circular Walks	Distance	Ascent	Allow
	Short	**1¾ miles**	**55m**	**1 hr**
		2.8km	180ft	
	Medium	**4¼ miles**	**140m**	**2½ hrs**
		6.8km	460ft	
	Longer	**6¾ miles**	**185m**	**3½ hrs**
		10.8km	610ft	
	Figure of eight walks			
	Short + Medium	**6 miles**	**195m**	**3½ hrs**
		9.6km	640ft	
	Short + Longer	**8½ miles**	**240m**	**4½ hrs**
		13.6km	790ft	
	Medium + Longer	**11 miles**	**325m**	**6 hrs**
		17.6km	1070ft	

(Walk Choices)

Special Interests	S	M	L	Local (Miles)
Outstanding viewpoints	✓	✓	✓	
Beech woodland	✓	✓	✓	
Turville Grange Grade II listed building			✓	
Stonor House Historic country house and private deer park			✓	
Next nearest pub: Bull and Butcher, Turville, RG9 6QU 01491 638283				3
Nearest town:				
Henley-on-Thames				5

Checkpoint grid references for GPS /Geocaching (Treasure Hunting)

Short	
①	SU 725 900
②	717 899
③	719 896
④	726 897

Medium	
①	SU 725 900
②	727 893
③	724 888
④	718 886
⑤	709 884
⑥	711 891
⑦	713 897
⑧	717 898

Longer			
①	SU 725 900	⑧	753 903
②	734 903	⑨	753 897
③	740 906	⑩	748 894
④	747 910	⑪	737 890
⑤	749 916	⑫	736 896
⑥	758 913	⑬	730 902
⑦	755 908		

Looking towards Turville

PISHILL SHORT WALK

1¾ miles (2.8km) • Ascent 55m (180ft) • Allow 1 hour

A lovely 'taster' walk; includes a meander high up through a beautiful beech woodland, picnic possibilities and a stunning view over Stonor Park.

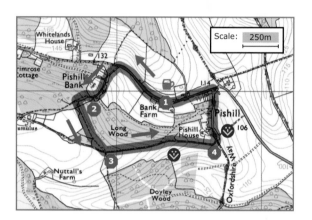

Checkpoints:

1 **Turn right** out of the car park at The Crown, and keep to the grass verge round a couple of bends in the road for 300m before **turning left** onto a footpath (metalled drive) at 'Pishill Bank' directing you to Maidensgrove. **Proceed uphill** on this metalled drive that becomes a wide track before narrowing to a footpath to the right of the house at the end of the drive. **Continue to walk uphill,** now through woodland and after 400m (¼ mile), as the hill is levelling out, **turn left** onto a waymarked footpath. *Note: there **is only one waymarked left turn** off this path, and if you look left along it, you'll see a white arrow on a tree.*

2 **Follow** white arrows on the trees, as the path meanders across the beech woodland more or less on the level (You've done the hard work getting up here!). At a crossing of footpaths, just inside the edge of the wood, **turn left.**

3 **Proceed downhill,** having glimpses over Stonor Park to your right Note: you can visit Stonor Park on the 'longer' walk from this location.

4 Coming out of the woods, **turn left** past 'Pishill House' and pause before reaching the church to look right for stunning views. Then descend to the main road and **turn left** for 200m back to the Crown.

Turville Valley from Idlecombe Wood

Stonor House

View from Stonor Park

PISHILL MEDIUM WALK

4¼ miles (6.8km) • Ascent 140m (460ft) • Allow 2½ hours

Quite a tough walk for its distance; provides four outstanding viewpoints over typically tranquil Chiltern landscapes as reward for your efforts.

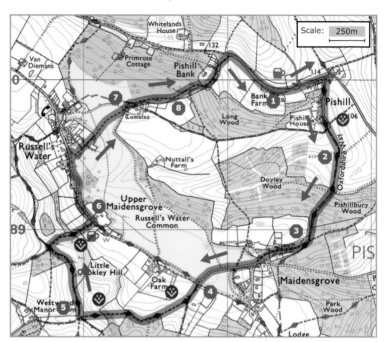

Checkpoints:

1 **Turn left** out of the car park at The Crown, and **turn right** (200m along the road) up to the church. Pass the church and continue ahead, with lovely views to your left. **Go through the gate ahead** on the 'Oxfordshire Way'. Do **NOT** turn right.

2 **Keep ahead** to the left hand side of the field which descends quite steeply and then rises, again very steeply, through 'Pishillbury Wood' to level out at the top.

3 **Turn right** off the Oxfordshire Way (**marked on a tree as footpath number PS19**). This takes you immediately out of the woodland between houses onto a quiet, metalled road. Pass a pond on your right and come to a more major road. **Turn right** onto it and after 200m arrive at a common, where you **continue on the road** until it bends sharply to the right.

4 **Leave the road at the bend** to continue ahead onto a track marked as a by- way as well as the Chiltern Way. After 100m **turn right** following the Chiltern Way, heading half right across a field. There is a good panoramic view here. **Meander at more or less the same level** through a woodland, before re-entering a field and descending quite sharply into another woodland. At the exit to this woodland there is a quite magnificent panorama and the tranquil setting is matched by a well-placed bench for reflection. It is then just a short descent across the field to the bottom right hand corner and then **turn right** at a junction of paths.

5 After about 400m (¼ mile) along the valley floor, and with a wood on your left, **turn right** onto a footpath that rises very steeply indeed, with a hedge on your left. On the way up, turn to your right and admire the view you're earning! At the top of the hill, go through a gate, up some steps and along a narrow enclosed path to come out on a road and **turn left**.

6 Along this road pass the 'Russell's Water' village sign and arrive at some houses before **turning sharply right** at a prominent footpath sign. Follow the path in the direction indicated. It bears left after a short while and, then, ignoring left and right possible turns, comes out onto a common. **Look to your right for a prominent house** and head across to it (no visible footpath).

7 Once there continue ahead to the left of that house on a track that leads shortly to a farm gate. **Don't go through the gate! Turn left** in front of it onto a footpath leading into the wood, following the white arrow directions provided, as the path meanders through on the level.

8 **Ignore a footpath forking to the right.** *Note: it is not clearly waymarked. It looks as though the main path goes to the right.* **Keep left** of the fork a**nd then descend steadily** to come out by the side of a house. **Follow the track,** which services the house, downhill to the main road, **turn right** and keep to the grass verges before arriving back at the starting point.

Bluebell Wood

PISHILL LONGER WALK

6¾ miles (10.8km) • Ascent 185m (610ft) • Allow 3½ hours

A beautiful walk through the best of Chiltern landscapes, including the deer park of Stonor House; some steep ascents rewarded by five outstanding viewpoints.

Checkpoints:

1 **Turn left** out of the car park at The Crown, and in 300m at the bend in the road, **turn left** onto the Oxfordshire Way footpath. After just 50m, **turn right** onto a narrow path between fence and hedge which climbs a little then crosses a track and continues ahead descending gradually, with fine views to your right.

2 **Continue ahead** over the cross path then climb steeply to reach a welcome seat to get your breath back and admire, again, wonderful panoramic views. **Continue ahead** and at a bend in the track 200m further on, **turn left** into a field.

3 **Cross** two fields to come out on a driveway between houses. **Cross the road** to a bus shelter and **turn to your right** and then **fork left** on the road. **Proceed ahead** for 125m and **turn left** onto a metalled drive for 200m to arrive at the front of 'Turville Grange'.

4 **Turn right** in front of the Grange and **turn left** beyond the house. **Cross** a stile and **turn left** to go ahead along the border fence of The Grange, passing its tennis courts. **Keep to the line** of this fence across the field (no visible footpath) and descend to the entrance to 'Idlecombe Wood'. **Follow the arrows** on the trees, going downhill and, at the edge of the wood, go down some steps and **turn right.**

5 Stay on this path, ignoring an immediate left turn and have a wonderful kilometre or so with great views across the valley to your left, before **bearing right** uphill.

6 Keep climbing through the woods for a over 400m (¼ mile), not taking left or right turns and coming out at 'Turville Court'.

7 **Turn right,** going along the boundary wall of Turville Court and **turning left** immediately afterwards onto a footpath that descends fairly steeply to the bottom left hand corner of a field. **Cross a stile,** then the road and another stile opposite. There is no visible footpath in this field, but **head in the direction shown on the footpath sign,** aiming for a prominent couple of trees slightly to your right on the opposite hedge. *Note: It is a good place to check the angle of the path on your map.* Before going through the gate at the top of the field, look back for more fine views all round.

8 After going through two consecutive gates, **keep to the right hand edge** of the field and **continue ahead** to a road. Cross the road and a couple of short fields to arrive onto a concrete road at 'Southend'. **Turn right** on the road, passing cottages to a T junction. **Turn left** along the road for 150m, before **turning right** off the road onto the Chiltern Way.

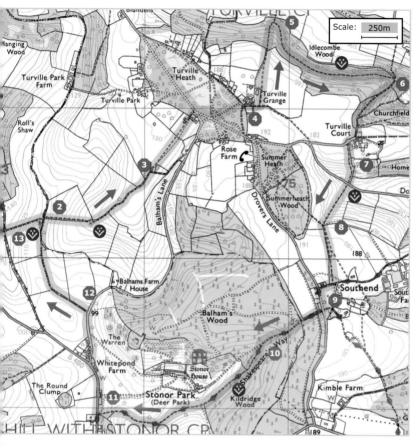

9 **Proceed directly ahead** through the woods following the white arrow marks, descending as you go. Lower down in the woods, **bear left** and enter 'Stonor Park' through a metal gate.

10 **Go ahead** for a kilometre through Stonor Park, keeping to the marked footpath and enjoying the views not only of Stonor House and gardens but of the setting in which it is placed. Eventually, you descend to come out of another metal gate onto a road.

11 **Turn right** on the road, walk along the grass verge for 300m and **fork right** at 'Whitepond Farm'. Pass a barn and, at a slight bend in the road, **turn left** onto a bridleway.

12 **Keep ahead** until you pass a barn on your left and then **turn left** beyond it at a cross path. Climb the gentle slope, looking left for fine views, to a cross track.

13 **Cross over the track** and descend on a narrow path to **turn left** at the end of it. Then, in 50m, **turn right** along the road, to arrive back at the start point

3. Turville

Start point: The Bull & Butcher, Turville, Henley-on-Thames, RG9 6QU 01491 638283. Customer parking at the pub.
Non-customer parking: nearby roadside

Turville is well known because of TV filming such as 'The Vicar of Dibley' and 'Chitty Chitty Bang Bang'. We not only the explore the village but also the lovely valley it nestles in and the surrounding hills and valleys.

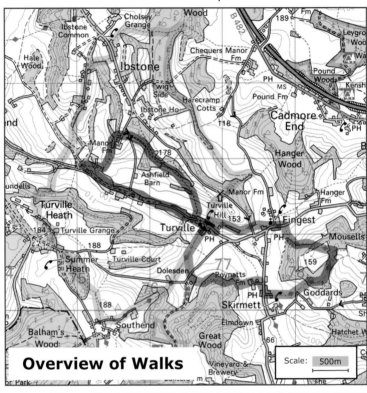

Overview of Walks

Scale: 500m

	Circular Walks	Distance	Ascent	Allow
Walk Choices	Short	**2¾ miles**	**60m**	**1½hrs**
		4.4km	195ft	
	Medium	**3½ miles**	**110m**	**2 hrs**
		5.6km	360ft	
	Longer	**7¼ miles**	**280m**	**3½ hrs**
		11.6km	1020ft	
	Figure of eight walks			
	Short + Medium	**6¼ miles**	**170m**	**3½ hrs**
		10km	555ft	
	Short + Longer	**10 miles**	**340m**	**5 hrs**
		16km	1215ft	
	Medium + Longer	**10¾ miles**	**390m**	**5½ hrs**
		17.2km	1380ft	

Special Interests	S	M	L	Local (Miles)
Outstanding viewpoints	✓	✓	✓	
Beech woodland	✓	✓	✓	
Turville Grange Grade II listed building			✓	
Turville Church	✓	✓	✓	
Turville Windmill (overlooking Turville village)	✓	✓	✓	
Ibstone Church	✓			
Next nearest pub: The Frog Skirmett RG9 6TG 01491 638996				1
Nearest town:				
Stokenchurch				4

Checkpoint grid references for GPS /Geocaching (Treasure Hunting)

Short

①	SU 767 912
②	763 918
③	757 923
④	754 918
⑤	758 915

Medium

①	SU 767 912
②	778 911
③	782 908
④	790 904
⑤	773 903
⑥	765 905

Longer

①	SU 767 912	⑧	748 923
②	763 904	⑨	751 931
③	758 900	⑩	755 935
④	752 903	⑪	765 938
⑤	748 910	⑫	773 917
⑥	745 913	⑬	770 915
⑦	748 919		

Looking across to Turville Hill

TURVILLE SHORT WALK

2¾ miles (4.4km) • Ascent 60m (195 feet) • Allow 1½ hours

A great 'starter' walk with two outstanding views across typical, beautiful and tranquil Chiltern landscapes, as well as a good view of the famous windmill.

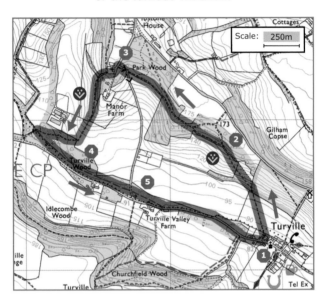

Checkpoints:

1 Coming out of the Bull and Butcher car park, **turn left,** walk just past the church and **turn right** onto a footpath between houses taking you up some steps and into a field. The path takes you half left across the field, and then upwards through a wooded area, then a field, as you climb quite steeply.

2 As the path reaches the woods at the top of the hill, pause, turn round, and admire a wonderful panorama. At this point, **do not** enter the wood. Rather, walk ahead along the edge of the wood, more or less on the level, until you come to the end of the field and **turn right** into the wood. Then, almost immediately, **turn left,** directed by a white arrow on a tree. Follow the white arrows on the trees, ignoring right hand paths, until you come to a road.

3 **Turn right** up the hill on the road and **turn left** after 100m into another road. It looks as though it's a dead end, but steps on the right take you into Ibstone Church's graveyard. **Continue on the same line as the steps** across the graveyard, descending into the woods beyond. Ahead is a white arrow on the tree directing you to descend sharply ahead downhill. Then **turn left** over a stile and admire a wonderful panorama before continuing downhill with great views all the way down!

4 **Enter a wood** and follow the white arrows on the trees looking out for a post with many markers on it; here, you turn **sharp left.** *Note: This is a good place to check the map to confirm the angle you have to take to get on the bridleway.* **Proceed ahead** on the bridleway to a narrow lane.

5 **Cross the lane** to keep on this bridleway, which runs in parallel with the road (on your right) going into Turville. It winds through a lovely beech wood, with glimpses of the windmill up to your left and eventually joins the main road (on your right) back to your starting point.

Windmill above village

Returning to Turville

TURVILLE MEDIUM WALK

3½ miles (5.6km) • Ascent 110m (360ft) • Allow 2 hours

One of my favourite walks; there is plenty of variety in height change, varied meadows and woodlands and outstanding views, particularly of the windmill.

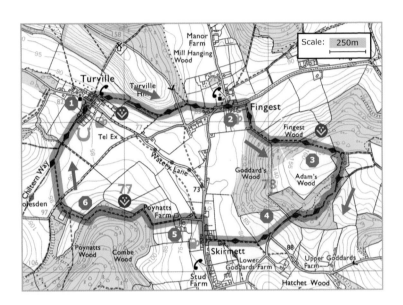

Checkpoints:

1 Coming out of the Bull and Butcher pub car park, **turn left** and then almost immediately **turn right** between houses to look up at the Windmill. Go through a gate and immediately **turn right** and traverse a grassy stretch with lovely views to your right. **Keep ahead,** coming onto a narrow path running round 'Turville Hill' which then crosses a road and, 50m further on, **bears right** down a path to come to the road at Fingest.

2 **Turn left** on the road and pass the church and, 100m past the Chequers pub, **turn right** onto a footpath. It sweeps around and up the right hand edge of the field to arrive at a bench which invites you to sit and admire a stunning panorama including Fingest Village (with church prominent) and, in the distance (some five miles away), the tower of the radio station at Stokenchurch.

3 **Go over the stile** to your right, through a short stretch of woodland, half left across a field and into another wood. On entering, **turn right** after 30m or so onto a path that descends through the woods and **forks left** on the Chiltern Way (tree marked with arrow and 'CW' = Chiltern Way).

4 **Come out of the wood** onto a track and **turn right**, after 100m, onto a footpath that leads directly down to Skirmett. **Turn right** on the road and then **turn left** onto a footpath 100m further on.

5 **Proceed ahead up the hill,** rounding a bend to your right as you ascend. The path then levels a little and you have another stunning panorama, including a great view of the Windmill. You bend left uphill for 100m through woodland before bearing right onto a level stretch, before descending. After 200m, **fork right** and come out of the woods. *Note: you could easily fork left here, but the public footpath you want is to the right.*

6 **Cross a short stretch of field** and go through a narrow wood to cross a road and enter a field. Follow the path, **bearing right** to join the Chiltern Way coming from your left, taking you back into Turville and your starting point.

Across Turville valley

TURVILLE LONGER WALK
7¼ miles (11.6km) • Ascent 280m (1020ft) • Allow 3½ hours

This is one of the tougher walks, with a lot of height changes - but also tremendous variety in valley and hill walking. There are many fine views and the one where you overlook Turville village from beside the windmill is a very satisfying way to end the walk.

Checkpoints:

1 Coming out of the Bull and Butcher car park, **turn left** past the pub, and **turn left** on the road before the church, joining the Chiltern Way going past the school. It becomes a footpath crossing a field (ignoring left and right turns) to a narrow lane

2 **Cross the lane** and climb steeply ahead. Look back before entering the wooded area for a good view of the windmill.

Passing 'Southend Farm', the path becomes a metalled road.

3 After about 300m, **fork right** on the road and, 50m beyond, **turn right** onto a footpath, following a hedge on the left hand side of the field. **Entering** the next field, **turn half left** and head, on the level, across to 'Summerheath Wood'. Turn round at the gate to admire a stunning panorama.

There are a number of unmarked paths spreading out into the wood from the entrance, so take the direction from the footpath arrow on the gate **(more or less straight on but slightly bearing right)**. *Note: this is a good place to look at your map, which shows the route of the path clearly through the woods.*

4 Now **follow the white arrows** on the trees, going always **straight ahead,** ignoring all side paths for 600m (nearly ½mile).

5 Coming out at a road, **turn left** along it, ignoring the road junction on your left, and **turn right** onto a footpath a few metres further on to come to 'Turville Grange'. **Turn left** along the front of the Grange and **continue ahead** on a bridleway past a barn and then **turn right** onto another bridleway.

6 It is quite a steep descent on a very stony bridleway through a wood to come out onto a narrow lane.

7 **Cross the lane,** go up a few steps and then around a tree to cross a stile into an open field. A wonderful panorama greets you, up and across the valley ahead. **Head straight across** the field, then a metalled track, and go through a few trees and then up a field steeply half left to a stile.

8 Turn round at the stile to enjoy yet another wonderful panorama. Then cross the stile and continue up to 'Hellcorner Farm', by which time the footpath has become a tarmac road.

9 Immediately after the farm, **turn right** onto a footpath which *quickly* forks (in a few paces). **Fork left** *as you enter the wood* descending into the valley before continuing in the same direction and through the swing gate up the other side to Ibstone.

10 **Turn left** on the road and after 150m **turn right** onto a footpath that starts to the left of a bungalow named Ravenscroft and descends to the right of 'Cholsey Grange' *(see map)*. You arrive at an open field, with a hedge on your left and good views to your right and continue the descent into woodland. Reaching the valley floor, **continue ahead** across a wide track onto a narrower path for 30m to **turn right** at a path 'T' junction.

11 Keep on this footpath along the valley floor, which merges with a bridleway coming from the right (and ignoring all turnings), for a total of over 2km (1½ miles) towards a road 'Chequers Lane'. *Note: The name 'Gravesend' is shown on the map where it meets the road.*

12 As the road comes into view (75m ahead of you) **turn sharp right** at a public footpath sign that takes you uphill through a field for 100m or so before entering woodland. Continue to climb quite steeply before joining a footpath coming from the left. On reaching the top of the hill (and a road) **turn right** on it, then almost immediately **turn left** through a gate onto the top of the hill with the windmill alongside you (in private grounds).

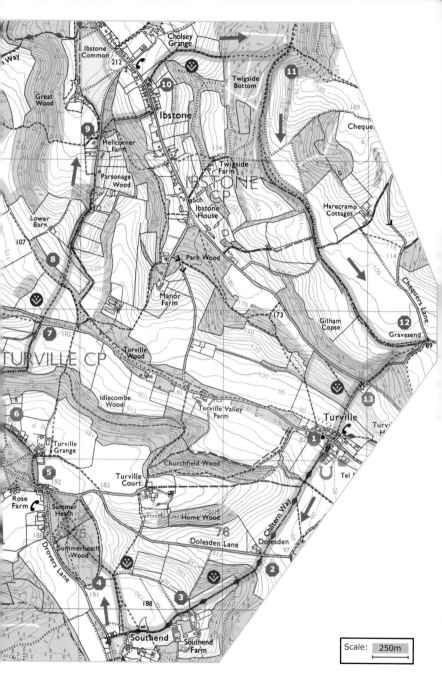

13 Here is your final great viewpoint position on the walk and the view is one of the most famous in the Chilterns. Magnificent!!! Now descend steeply into Turville and the end of your walk.

4. Piddington

Start point: The Dashwood Arms, Old Oxford Road, Piddington, Bucks HP14 3BH 01494 881488. **Parking:** nearby roadside.

Apart from the starter walk, the others are quite tough but extremely varied in landscape, with incredible views providing reward for effort. A delightful set of walks.

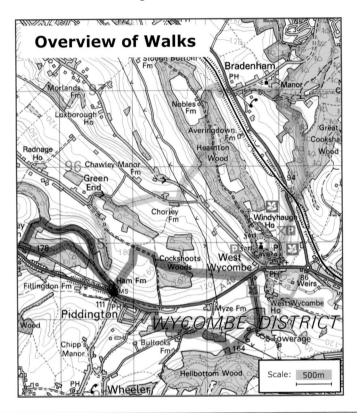

	Circular Walks	Distance	Ascent	Allow
	Short	**2¼ miles**	**70m**	**1½hrs**
		3.6km	230ft	
	Medium	**3½ miles**	**175m**	**2 hrs**
		5.6km	575ft	
	Longer	**7 miles**	**290m**	**4 hrs**
		11.2km	1050ft	
Walk Choices	**Figure of eight walks**			
	Short + Medium	**5¾ miles**	**245m**	**3½ hrs**
		9.2km	805ft	
	Short + Longer	**9¼ miles**	**360m**	**5½ hrs**
		14.8km	1215ft	
	Medium + Longer	**10½ miles**	**465m**	**6 hrs**
		16.8km	1625ft	

Special Interests	S	M	L	Local (Miles)
Outstanding viewpoints		✓	✓	
Beech woodland	✓	✓	✓	
Bradenham Manor Benjamin Disraeli's father's house, now a conference centre.			✓	
West Wycombe House House and grounds open to public			✓	
Mausoleum and Church			✓	
Hellfire Caves Café and caves			✓	
Next nearest pub: The Swan Inn, West Wycombe HP14 3AE 01494 527031				1½
Nearest town:				
High Wycombe				4

Checkpoint grid references for GPS /Geocaching (Treasure Hunting)

Short	
❶	SU 808 943
❷	797 953
❸	797 948
❹	804 946

Medium	
❶	SU 808 943
❷	810 949
❸	817 946
❹	826 945
❺	827 938
❻	822 938
❼	813 938

Longer			
❶	SU 808 943	❽	829 968
❷	807 951	❾	832 955
❸	804 955	❿	830 948
❹	813 956	⓫	826 946
❺	819 959	⓬	817 946
❻	820 968	⓭	810 949
❼	824 971		

Looking over West Wycombe

PIDDINGTON SHORT WALK

2¼ miles (3.6 km) • Ascent 70m (230ft) • Allow 1½ hours

A relatively easy 'starter' walk along a valley past a farm, then into and up through a beautiful beech wood; re-joining the track eventually to pass the farm again back to the starting point.

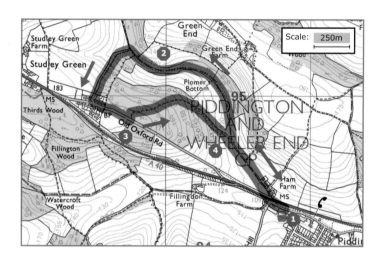

Checkpoints:

1 From the Old Oxford Road, Dashwood Arms Pub (kerbside parking) **cross the main road** and **proceed ahead** on a bridleway that passes 'Ham Farm'. **Keep ahead** on the bridleway along the valley floor for over 1km, passing between fields and entering a lovely beech wood.

2 **Turn left** onto another bridleway 20m after passing the Bottom Wood Nature Reserve information board (on your right). The path rises sharply **straight ahead** just inside the woodland, allowing glimpses of a field through the beech trees. It is some 400m to the top of the hill where it meets a road (Old Oxford Road). **Turn left** onto the road for 300m before **turning left** onto a footpath.

3 **Continue ahead** through a wood, gradually losing height for 700m (nearly ½ mile) before coming out of the wood and meeting the bridle way you came along earlier.

4 **Turn right** onto the bridleway and return to Piddington and your starting point.

West Wycombe Hill

View from Hearnton Wood

Church (with golden ball) and Mausoleum

PIDDINGTON MEDIUM WALK

3½ miles (5.6km) • Ascent 175m (575ft) • Allow 2 hours

Quite a tough walk including two quite steep ascents; includes beautiful views towards the Golden-balled church and Mausoleum at West Wycombe.

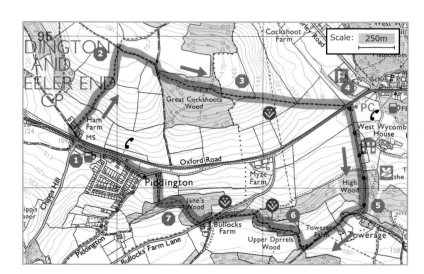

Checkpoints:

1 From the Old Oxford Road, Dashwood Arms Pub (kerbside parking) **cross** the main road and enter the bridleway. **Turn right** onto a footpath after 75m, at Ham Farm and **ascend** quite steeply for nearly half a mile. As the footpath levels out at the top of the hill, **go over the stile** (to keep to the left of the final fence) to arrive at a cross-path and **turn right.**

2 **Cross** a 250m wide field, keeping to the right hand edge, to **turn right** onto a bridleway, coming in from the left. 50m on, **turn left** into 'Great Cockshoots Wood' and traverse the 400m (¼ mile) wide wood more or less on the level.

3 Coming out of the wood the path **bears to the right** initially but after 50m or so, **bears left** to continue ahead downhill. For the next 800m (½ mile) you are treated to a wonderful panoramic view as you cross the middle of two fields.

4 **Arriving** at the A40 Oxford Road, **cross it** and proceed straight ahead up a minor metalled road, for nearly 800m (½ mile), entering 'High Wood'.

5 At the top of the hill, **turn right** and continue ahead on the level. 250m past 'Towerage Farm', as the track begins to descend slightly, **fork right** at two telephone poles onto a footpath for 60m before **turning sharp right** at a cross-path. You now cross a field to enter 'Upper Dorrels Wood'.

6 Turning **half left** as you enter the wood, **descend** gradually.
Coming out of the wood keep straight on with the hedge on your left to **cross** a field, with lovely views to your right. Join a wide track going slightly uphill, and take a footpath on your right to arrive at a metalled road ('Bullocks Farm Lane'). **Turn left** and proceed along the road for 100m, with fine views to your right, and then **turn right** onto a footpath into 'Jane's Wood'.

7 After 50m, **fork right** to **descend** through the wood and then **cross** a field to arrive at a metalled road. **Turn left** onto the road to come back to the start point.

Beech Wood

PIDDINGTON LONGER WALK

7 miles (11.2km) • Ascent 290m (1050ft) • Allow 4 hours

One of the toughest walks in this Guide, but filled with interest on the way. There are outstanding views, tranquil beech woods and you pass Bradenham Manor, the Mausoleum, Hellfire Caves and West Wycombe House.

Checkpoints:

1 From the Old Oxford Road, Dashwood Arms Pub (kerbside parking) **cross** the main road and enter the bridleway opposite. **Continue ahead** for 200m past Ham Farm to **turn right** onto a footpath in a gap in the hedge. **Ascend** quite steeply through a field to go through a short strip of woodland.

2 Coming out of the woodland near the top of the hill, **turn sharp left** along the edge of a field. ***Now take care!*** The path (which may not be clearly marked) does not curve upwards round with the field, rather goes **straight ahead.** It comes out at a crossing track after 250m (where there are good views to your left), and you cross a stile in front of you then head straight up across the field (no visible path). Go to the other side of the field and **turn left** in front of the hedges. **Proceed ahead,** with the hedge on your right, to arrive at 'Green End Farm'. **Turn right** through a gate onto a path that takes you to the front of the farm and **turn left** on its drive to arrive at a road.

3 **Turn right** onto the road ('Hatch Lane'). Then, almost immediately, **turn right** off the road onto a footpath that follows the road but from inside the hedge. The path goes right and then continues ahead as the road turns left. 300m further it emerges from 'Chawley Wood' to **cross** two fields **half right** (*check the direction on the map*) and come out onto 'Bottom Road' and **turn right.**

4 300m along the road, **turn left** off the road onto a path that crosses, in quick succession, two roads and three fields to ascend steeply to enter 'Hearnton Wood'. Before entering the wood, turn round to admire a wonderful panorama. *Note: A convenient bench is there for a well-earned rest as you admire the view!*

5 On entering the wood, the path **ascends** quite steeply for a further 150m, **crosses a clearing** and then more or less on the level **proceeds ahead** for another 150m to come to a distinctive cross track and **turn left. Proceed ahead,** on the level, to arrive at 'Nobles Farm' and **turn right.**

6 This path goes **sharply downhill** and **turns right** through a gate at the foot of the hill to continue ahead with the hedges on your right. 200m on, **turn left** with the path as it goes under the railway line and comes to the main A4010 road at 'Bradenham'. Cross the road, **turn right** and then, almost immediately, **turn left** past the pub into Bradenham Wood Lane.

7 After 125m, cross the road onto a track that runs around the cricket square and heads to the right of the Church and 'Bradenham Manor'. Keep on this track, passing Bradenham Manor on your left until you come to the corner of its high boundary wall. Here is a signpost with multiple directions. Ahead of you is a fork in the track you are on, but you take **neither** fork. Rather, you **turn right** onto a footpath heading straight into woodland. ('Pimlock's Wood'.)

8 **Proceed ahead** through the wood, climbing gradually. After 75m ***take care!*** You need to **bear left** at a possible fork to arrive, 30m on, at a post with a yellow arrow on it. **Bear right** around the post and continue ascending for 200m before levelling out. **Keep ahead** ignoring turnings and staying more or less on the level. After 400m (¼ mile) a track joins from your left (shown on the map just above 'Kit's Wood'). **Continue ahead** on the level, for 250m before the track bears to the left and you **turn right** off it at a footpath sign. **Descend** through the woods for 400m to the railway track and **turn right.**

9 **Proceed ahead** for 200m to the main A4010 road, **cross it** and **turn left** under the railway bridge on the main road footpath.

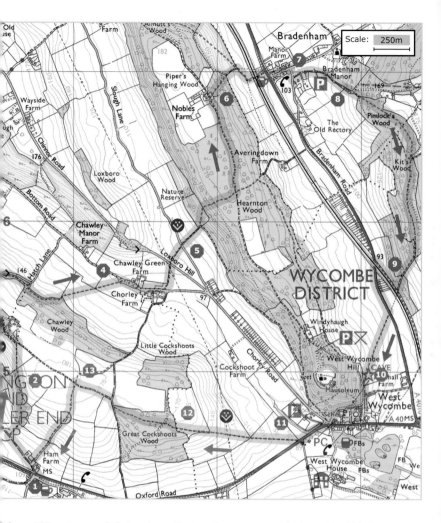

After 400m **turn right** onto a footpath to proceed ahead half left
across a field, aiming for the top left hand corner.

10 Coming out onto a metalled road, **turn left** and then curve right
with the road to pass the Hellfire Caves on your right and then a
school on your left to descend to the main A40 road. **Turn right** on
the A40 (there is a good roadside path) for 200m and **turn right** onto
a footpath.

11 You now climb steadily uphill **half left** across two open fields for
800m (½ mile) to enter 'Great Cockshoots Wood'. On the way,
keep pausing to look round at a wonderful panoramic view.

12 Enter the wood and cross it more or less on the level to arrive
at a bridleway and **turn right** onto it. After 50m, **turn left** for
250m to come to a cross path and **turn left.**

13 **Descend sharply** to 'Ham Farm' and **turn left** onto the
bridleway for the last 100m or so back to the start point.

5. Stokenchurch

Start point: Kings Hotel, Oxford Road, Stokenchurch, Bucks HP14 3TA 01494 609090
Public parking at the hotel or nearby off main road kerbside.

A walk through the Wormsley Estate, through Yoesden Nature Reserve and visit up to eight outstanding viewpoints to pause and ponder on the tranquillity of the whole, makes this one of my favourite locations for all seasons.

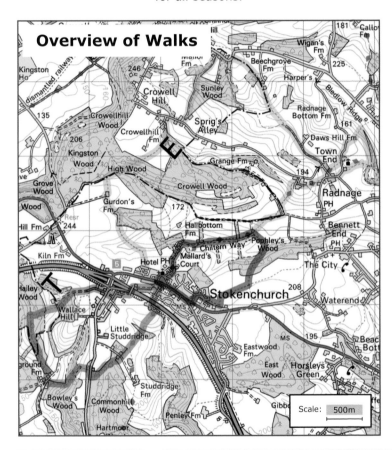

Overview of Walks

Bluebell Wood

Special Interests	S	M	L	Local (Miles)
Outstanding viewpoints	✓	✓	✓	
Beech woodland	✓	✓	✓	
Wormsley Estate (Getty family)		✓		
Yoesden Nature Reserve (inc. wild flower meadow)			✓	
Radnage Church 13th Century			✓	
Next nearest pub: Many refreshment facilities within Stokenchurch				0

Checkpoint grid references for GPS / Geocaching (Treasure Hunting)

Short	
❶	SU 760 964
❷	768 960
❸	773 963
❹	773 969
❺	766 967

Medium	
❶	SU 760 964
❷	757 955
❸	750 952
❹	744 950
❺	742 958
❻	751 963

Longer			
❶	SU 760 964	❽	770 993
❷	766 968	❾	763 984
❸	777 973	❿	758 979
❹	780 977	⓫	753 976
❺	789 979	⓬	754 970
❻	787 982	⓭	758 964
❼	777 984		

	Circular Walks	Distance	Ascent	Allow
Walk Choices	Short	**2½ miles**	**50m**	**1 hr**
		4km	165ft	
	Medium	**3¾ miles**	**170m**	**2 hrs**
		6km	555ft	
	Longer	**7½ miles**	**310m**	**4 hrs**
		12km	1115ft	
	Figure of eight walks			
	Short + Medium	**6¼ miles**	**220m**	**3 hrs**
		10km	720ft	
	Short + Longer	**10 miles**	**360m**	**5 hrs**
		16km	1280ft	
	Medium + Longer	**11¼ miles**	**480m**	**6 hrs**
		18km	1670ft	

STOKENCHURCH SHORT WALK

2½ miles (4km) • Ascent 50m (165ft) • Allow 1 hour

A very gentle walk mainly across open fields, but also through a beech wood; also outstanding views across a valley.

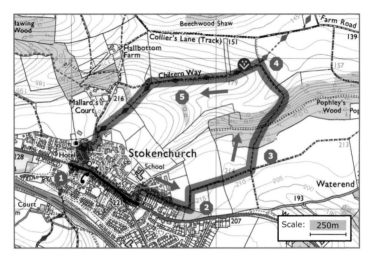

Checkpoints:

1 Imagine coming out of the front door of the Kings Hotel. **Turn left.** Walk along the roadside footpath for just over a quarter of a mile, passing George Road to **turn left** into the next road you come to, The Coppice (a cul-de-sac). Continue ahead through the cul-de-sac onto a footpath that comes, shortly, to a 'T' junction of paths and you **turn right. Proceed ahead** on the path, with a housing estate boundary on your left, for some 300m before turning sharp left around the end of a playing field.

2 **Continue ahead** on the level for 150m when the path turns right. Again on the level, **continue ahead** on a narrow path with a field on your right, to come through the hedge at the end of the field into a wide, open field. **Continue ahead** for 200m until you come to a cross path, on which you **turn left.**

3 **Cross** the field on the level and descend steadily through 'Pophley's Wood', following white arrows on the trees. As you come out of the wood, keep to the right hand side of a field, still descending and then shortly rising, levelling out and then descending to join a track coming from your left. Almost immediately **turn left** up steps onto a footpath that crosses the track (thus joining the Chiltern Way).

4 At first, you **proceed ahead**, with a hedge on your left, for 400m (¼ mile) and fantastic panoramic views all along the way. You then come to a small gap in the hedge and a Chiltern Way sign directs you through the gap.

5 Now you **proceed ahead** (still following the Chiltern Way)with the hedge on your right along a wide track until, ahead of a gate, it bears off half left across a field, and passes through into the next field. Here you have some trees on your right as you go ahead to a metalled lane and **turn left** onto it. This lane brings you back to the centre of Stokenchurch and your starting point.

Looking towards Radnage Church

Beech wood in Wormsley Park

STOKENCHURCH MEDIUM WALK

3¾ miles (6km) • Ascent 170m (555ft) • Allow 2 hours

A delightful, but quite strenuous walk through the Wormsley Estate, with tremendous variety of ascents and descents through beech woods and fields.

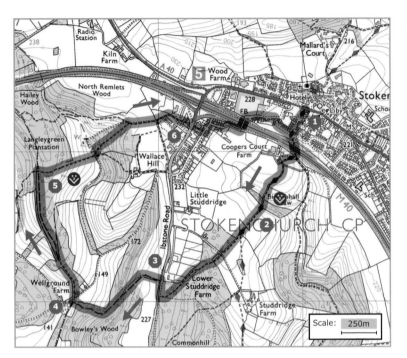

Checkpoints:

1 Imagine stepping out of the front of the Kings Hotel. **Head straight** across the road and continue (with the Fleur de Lis pub to your right) to descend Coopers Court Road and go under the M40 motorway, following the Chiltern Way. **Turn right** the other side to ascend and continue ahead on the Chiltern Way. Long distance views are available to your left, as you walk with the hedge on your right before going downhill and then back up through a small wood.

2 **Coming out** of the wood continue ascending before **proceeding ahead,** more or less on the level, across two fields (with hedges on your right) and across a drive into another field. On entering 'Commonhill Wood' follow arrows on the trees as you first **wind downhill** for 75m before then winding back up for some 300m to arrive at a road, and **turn right.**

3 **Turn left off the road** after 100m onto a footpath that is on the level for 100m before descending steeply through 'Bowley's Wood', to the valley floor and 'Wellground Farm'.

4 **Cross the track** and head uphill on a bridleway, through 'Langleygreen Plantation'. It is a steady climb, following arrows on the trees, for nearly 1km (just over ½ mile) to a cross-path (marked again, with arrows on a tree) and **turn right.** *Note: 200m or so before the turning, the path levels out.*

5 **Ascend** for a short distance, following white arrows on the trees, before **winding down** through 'Langleygreen Plantation'. As you come out of the wood, turn left over the stile into a field (with very good all round views) continuing in the same direction to the valley floor. **Fork left** on the footpath crossing the valley floor and **follow the arrows** on trees to take you steeply back up the other side. Coming out of the wood, **turn right**, cross a stile and then **proceed straight ahead** across a field and through a small industrial estate to arrive at a drive. **Cross the drive** and continue on a wide track between houses to a road.

6 **Continue ahead** by crossing the road and following a footpath to another road and **turn left** onto it. After 75m, **turn right** onto an un-metalled road (called Green Lane) that takes you to the pedestrian bridge over the M40. **Turn right** on the other side of the motorway to return to the starting point.

STOKENCHURCH LONGER WALK

7½ miles • (12km) • Ascent 310m (1115ft) • Allow 4 hours

There are six outstanding viewpoints on this lovely walk. It crosses so many gently undulating hills and valleys that you are surprised to find you've ascended some 1,000ft (310m) in height by the end of the walk. On the way, you pass Radnage church and go through Yoesden Nature Reserve with wonderful views over Radnage.

Checkpoints:

1 From the Kings Hotel car park go around the back of the hotel and go down a metalled track beside the Royal Oak pub. 150m down the lane, turn off ahead of a 'private road' sign onto the Chiltern Way footpath. Head **half left** across a field to walk along the right hand side of a row of trees and through a gate into another field. **Turn left** to continue on the Chiltern Way dipping slightly before rising and joining a wide track with a hedge on your left hand side. Just before the track itself turns left, **turn left** through the hedge, still on the Chiltern Way.

2 You now have the hedge on your right, with lovely views to the left and front. Continue ahead, for 800m (½ mile) to **go down** a few steps and **cross straight over** a wide track. This path leads you down to the foot of the valley where you meet a wide track on which you **turn right.** Proceed ahead for 200m to come to a metalled track and **turn left.**

3 After 100m, **turn right** onto a footpath (still the Chiltern Way) to head uphill **half left** aiming to the right of a telegraph pole; to then continue the walk uphill on the right hand side of the field. *Note: turn round occasionally to admire a panoramic view.* **Turn right** through the gap at the top of the field and almost immediately (within 20m) **turn right** through a gate, still on the Chiltern Way and keep to the right hand side of a short field. Go **across a drive** into a small estate, and

turn right onto another drive that goes between houses and comes off a concrete track into a field.

4 **Go ahead,** keeping to the left hand side of the field (still on the Chiltern way), with fine views across the valley to your right, to **descend** 200m to a road (Horseshoe Road) and turn left onto it. 100m down the road, turn right at a junction (onto Town End Road), passing a prominent house with three garages, and then **turn left** at a road 'T' junction. 100m on, as the road bends to the left, **turn right** off it onto a footpath. Proceed ahead through two gates and keep ahead until you meet the left hand edge of a wood ('Yoesden Wood', on your right). The Chiltern Way goes straight up the hill, but you (after going through a gate) **turn sharp left** off it onto a permissive path leading into the meadow of the Nature Reserve.

5 The permissive path heads upwards, **half left** towards a wood, and you are now standing in a wild flower meadow. Walk along the top of the flower meadow, **just below the tree line,** passing two information boards about the location, as well as enjoying fine views to your left. When you reach the other end of the field, **turn sharp left downhill** (steeply), with the hedge on your right, cross two fields and come to a road and **turn left** on it.

6 300m down the road, opposite the entrance drive to the church, **turn right** and cross a field (approximately 150m) to arrive at another road on which you **turn right.** 100m on, as the road turns left, go ahead onto a metalled bridleway (also signed to a 'Vineyard'). When you arrive at the end of the metalled track, continue the bridleway ahead to the left of the entrance to the vineyard. 400m (¼ mile) beyond the vineyard, **turn right** off the bridleway over a stile onto a footpath heading across the middle of a field.

7 **Keep ahead** on this footpath that goes through a hedge gap and then climbs quite steeply (with wide views all the way up the hill) to the top right hand corner of the next field. It then **continues ahead** through a small wood, **crosses** another field to the top right hand corner, coming to a road on which you **turn left.**

8 250m along the road, **turn left** onto a bridleway (signposted to 'Sprig's Alley') through a wooded area that starts on the level but then descends quite quickly to the valley floor. It then goes up the edge of 'Venus Wood' to 'Sprig's Alley', where you **turn right** onto a road.

9 After 200m, **turn left** onto a bridleway (concrete drive entrance to a farm) and **continue ahead** on the bridleway to the left of the drive, entering 'Crowell Wood'. *Note: this bridleway can get very muddy in wintertime, and a 'side-path' runs beside it on the bank.* After 250m **fork right** onto a bridleway and after 50m, **turn right** onto a footpath that leaves the wood (through a gate) to climb up and across a field. The field is about 400m (¼ mile) across and then enters 'High Wood'.

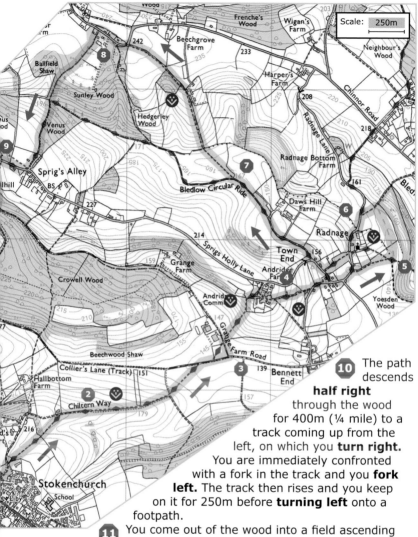

10 The path descends **half right** through the wood for 400m (¼ mile) to a track coming up from the left, on which you **turn right.** You are immediately confronted with a fork in the track and you **fork left.** The track then rises and you keep on it for 250m before **turning left** onto a footpath.

11 You come out of the wood into a field ascending for a while before passing in front of some buildings ('Gurdon's Farm'). **Continue ahead,** descending to your left onto the floor of 'Stockfield Wood'. 75m into the wood **turn right** to go sharply uphill through the wood to come out onto a field.

12 Go ahead on the **right hand side** of the field. After 100m, there are great views to your left as the path itself slopes downhill **half left** to **enter** a second field. Here, you keep to the **right hand side** going back uphill through a band of trees. At the top of the hill, **turn right** into a field and go ahead with the hedge on your left hand side, more or less on the level, to arrive onto a housing estate.

13 **Turn left** as you come to the road, having passed between properties, and then **turn right** at the 'T' junction ahead. Within 40m along this road **turn left** onto footpath, again between properties, to come out in the centre of Stokenchurch and back at the Kings Hotel.

6. Great Kingshill

Start point: Public car park, The Common Great Kingshill, High Wycombe, Bucks HP15 6EN. Pub opposite: The Red Lion, Missenden Road, Great Kingshill, High Wycombe, Bucks HP15 6EB 01494 711262

This location has a lot to offer with a strong contrast between the walks. Ranging from very flat (medium walk) to dramatic viewpoints on the short and longer walks. A good location to choose a half day walk and visit Hughenden Manor for half a day, too.

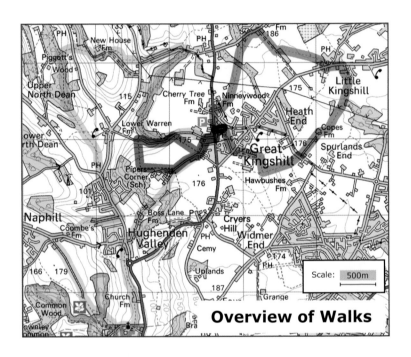

Overview of Walks

	Circular Walks	Distance	Ascent	Allow
	Short	**2 miles**	**45m**	**1 hr**
		3.2km	150ft	
	Medium	**3¾ miles**	**Negligible**	**1½ hrs**
		6km		
Walk Choices	Longer	**8¼ miles**	**243m**	**4 hrs**
		13.2km	805ft	
	Figure of eight walks			
	Short + Medium	**5¾ miles**	**45m**	**2½ hrs**
		9.2km	150ft	
	Short + Longer	**10¼ miles**	**288m**	**5 hrs**
		16.4km	955ft	
	Medium + Longer	**12 miles**	**243m**	**5½ hrs**
		19.2km	805ft	

Special Interests	S	M	L	Local (Miles)
Outstanding viewpoints	✓		✓	
Beech woodland	✓	✓	✓	
Hughenden Manor Country House of Benjamin Disraeli. Open to public (house and gardens)			✓	
Next nearest pub: White Lion Cryers Hill HP15 6JP 01494 713900				½
Nearest Town:				
High Wycombe				4

Checkpoint grid references for GPS /Geocaching (Treasure Hunting)

Short

①	SU 877 982
②	871 976
③	865 980
④	870 980

Medium

①	SU 877 982
②	883 976
③	890 980
④	894 990
⑤	886 992
⑥	880 993
⑦	878 986

Longer

①	SU 877 982	⑨	861 976
②	871 976	⑩	855 984
③	867 970	⑪	855 992
④	864 964	⑫	863 992
⑤	865 956	⑬	866 990
⑥	860 957	⑭	874 991
⑦	854 966	⑮	870 980
⑧	863 970		

Mass of Buttercups

GREAT KINGSHILL SHORT WALK

2 miles (3.2km) • Ascent 45m (150ft) • Allow 1 hour

A starter walk with an outstanding view that you reach on the level, before descending quite sharply to turn right and make your way back to the start point.

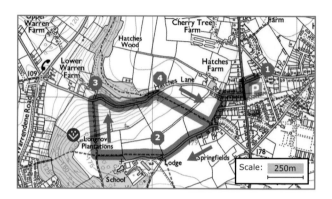

Checkpoints:

1 From the car park, **turn right** up to the main road, then **turn left** along it and cross the road to enter Hatches Lane. After 200m, at a 'road narrows' sign, **turn left** onto a footpath that passes some cottages and becomes narrower. **Continue** past the end of a cul-de-sac and, upon reaching a lane, **turn right** onto it. **Proceed ahead** on the level for 400m (¼ mile) to the 'Lodge' (entrance to a school) and **turn right** onto a footpath.

2 In the field, immediately **turn left** to walk along the inside of the hedge, on the level, passing the school grounds on your left. On your right and ahead there are good views. After 400m (¼ mile), at the end of the school grounds, you **come to a cross path** and **turn right** to head for a gate in the middle of the field. There is a wonderful panoramic view here and you could linger to admire it. **Carry on ahead,** descending steeply to **turn right** onto Hatches Lane.

3 This is a narrow, quiet lane, which rises quite steeply and after 400m (¼ mile) **turn right** off the road onto a footpath into a field.

4 There may be no visible path, and you need to head straight up the field to the left of the trees in front of you (in the direction shown on the signpost). *Note: It is also a good time to confirm the direction of the path by looking at your map.* Arriving at the top of the hill **go ahead** through a gate into the next field, keeping to the right hand edge. At the end of that field, **go through a gate** and **turn left** onto the footpath you started the walk on earlier. **Go ahead,** passing the cul-de-sac to come to Hatches Lane and **turn right** to come back to your starting point.

Looking out across Hughenden Valley

Overlooking Hughenden Manor church

Looking towards Naphill

GREAT KINGSHILL MEDIUM WALK

3¾ miles (6.0km) • Ascent negligible • Allow 1½ hours

A very easy walk, more or less on the flat, over fields and through woodland.

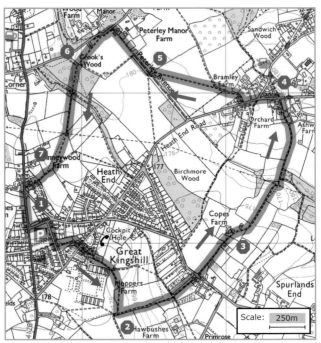

Checkpoints:

1 From the car park, **cross straight over** the common to go round beyond the children's playground and come out at the top corner of the common onto a road and **turn right.** Almost immediately, **turn left** and proceed ahead across a short stretch of green to **cross** a road between houses and continue on a footpath. This winds between properties before coming out onto a wide field and **immediately fork right** at a footpath junction. **Continue ahead,** through a gate and across another field to a footpath 'T' junction and **turn left.**

2 The path descends for a few hundred metres, with good views right and left, before coming back up to a cross path. **Cross straight over** to go along a narrow footpath with high fences to arrive at a road, which you **cross onto a drive. Proceed ahead** and then come off the drive onto a footpath **to the right of** the entrance to 'Copes Farm'.

3 This path **continues ahead** for 1km across several meadows and a thicket, always keeping to the left hand edge and mostly on the level. It comes out onto a road, with the Kingshill Baptist Church on your left. **Cross the road** and **turn left** on the pavement.

4 **Cross a road ahead,** that joins from the right, and a 100m beyond, **turn right** into a cul de sac (Shepherds Gate) and

continue through onto a footpath that comes to a wide field. **Proceed ahead** for 50m and **fork left** at a footpath junction and follow the edge of a wood-fenced enclosure, with wide views all round, to the far corner of the field.

5 **Coming out** of the field onto a wide track, **turn right** onto a bridleway for 400m (¼ mile) to pass a farm shop, and come to the entrance to 'Peterley Manor Farm'. **Turn sharp left at the gatepost** to join a footpath before the road, heading slightly left to pass the back of a house in the direction of 'Crook's Wood'.

6 Enter **'Crook's Wood'** and **proceed straight ahead** for 200m having ignored left and right turns, to come out the other side of the wood into a field. The path, clearly identified, continues ahead on the same line. You then have to **go through a gap** into the next field and **continue in the same direction** over a field with no visible path, aiming to the left of a large barn. *Note: it's worth seeing the line on your map.* You end in the corner of the field and cross a stile to come to a small housing estate.

7 **Continue ahead,** crossing the estate road, and entering a short path to the main road ahead. **Cross over** and **turn left** on the roadside path. Stay on this side of the road for approximately 350m to then **re-cross the road** to arrive back at the starting point.

....

GREAT KINGSHILL LONGER WALK

8¼ miles (13.2km) • Ascent 243m (805ft) • Allow 4 hours

Quite a challenging walk with a reasonably high ascent content- hence the six outstanding viewpoints achieved. The walk is very varied, passing through fields, woodland and meadows and also passes Hughenden Manor.

Checkpoints:

1 From the car park **turn right** up to the main road, **turn left** along it, and then **turn right** into Hatches Lane. After 200m, at a 'road narrows' sign, **turn left** onto a footpath that passes some cottages and becomes narrower. **Continue** past the end of a cul-de-sac and upon reaching a lane, **turn right** onto it. **Proceed ahead** for 400m (¼ mile) to come to some school gates and **bear left,** staying on the metalled road.

2 The lane shortly becomes an un-metalled track and descends for 300m with some fine views between the trees to the left. It passes Boss Lane Farm and becomes metalled again.

3 **Continue ahead** on the lane until it comes to the main road at a roundabout. **Turn left** on a good pavement along the main road for 50m to a bus stop shelter and then **cross over** to **go up a few steps** and **immediately turn left** onto a footpath that runs behind the houses. After 200m it comes out onto a wide field.

4 **Go ahead** along the foot of the valley for the next kilometre without turning left or right. *Note: check your map where the line of the path is clearly shown.* After crossing several fields, with fine views on both sides of the valley, you go through a gate into the grounds of 'Hughenden Manor' and **turn right.**

5 **Proceed up** the metalled road for 175m and **turn right** onto the footpath (signed Naphill) that runs along the outside edge of a wood. The path climbs for about 350m basically circumnavigating Hughenden Manor. There are fine views to the right. Ignore all left and right paths to come out at the main car park, right at the top of the hill. **Turn half right** on a wide track, keeping the car park and hedge on your left.

6 **Keep ahead** on this track, without turning left or right, for 1km with occasional wide views over and between hedges. You then pass a few buildings/ houses before coming to a main road.

7 **Cross the road and turn right** to walk along the other side (with good pavements). After 200m, beyond a row of houses and opposite Gentian Cottage, **turn left** into a field and go **half right** across it (with fine views ahead of you). **Continue ahead** descending through a wood to arrive on an un-metalled road, with houses down both sides.

8 At the bottom of the road is a main road. **Cross and turn left** along the opposite pavement. **Keep ahead** for nearly 650m to come to the Harrow Pub.

9 **Go round** the pub into Warrendene Road and **immediately cross over the road** to **join a footpath** going ahead across the field. *Note: check your map to confirm the line of the path.* **Go ahead** through a gate into the next field, always climbing. Pause occasionally to see a wide panoramic view. As the path levels out **enter** 'Piggott's Wood'.

10 **Immediately turn left** on entering the wood *Note: there are no footpath direction arrows, but **DO NOT** go straight ahead here.* After 75m along a well waymarked path, **turn right,** to descend for just 50m and **turn left** at a path junction. *Note: This is a good place to confirm with the map!* The prominent path you're now on crosses the wood more or less at the same level for 650m, and then comes to a path 'T' junction (again well waymarked). **Turn right** here.

11 **Descend steeply** through the wood and come out onto a field. **Continue ahead, cross a road** to join another path and climb very steeply **half right** up the hill, not forgetting to pause and admire the panoramic views. **Cross a stile** into another field and then over another stile to **turn right** onto a metalled drive. **Stay on the drive** as it sweeps round to the left and up, to level out between properties. **Turn off the drive** beyond the properties to **cross a stile on the left side of the drive** and then **turn sharp right** along the fence. *Note: you can see clearly the line of the path on the map.*

12 The path, always clinging to the right hand edge of the field, sweeps downhill to the bottom right hand corner. **Come out onto a road** on which you **turn right.**

13 **Almost immediately, turn left** onto Perks Lane and stay on it for 800m (½ mile). It goes uphill between houses and then curves sharply to the right, still climbing. Shortly afterwards, **turn right** off the road into 'Longfield Wood'.

14 You now have a lovely, long (over a kilometre) walk through a typical Chilterns beech wood, more or less on the level, with

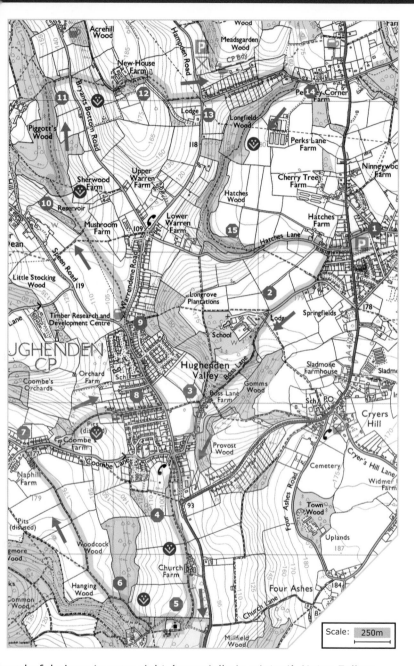

wonderful views to your right (especially in winter!) *Note: Follow the arrows on the trees, even when they direct you downwards for a short distance.* The path undulates quite comfortably and ends at a property's front gates on your left.

15 **Go ahead** down the property's drive to come out onto 'Hatches Lane' **and turn left** along it for 600m back into Gt Kingshill and your starting point.

7. Lower Cadsden

Start point: The Plough at Cadsden, Longdown Hill, Princes Risborough, Bucks HP27 0NB 01844 343302. Customer parking at pub. **Non-customer parking:** Limited (5 or 6 cars) on entrance road to pub (or up hill off road).

These lovely walks visit Chequers (the Prime Minister's country residence) as well as providing fine views from Coombe and Whiteleaf Hills.

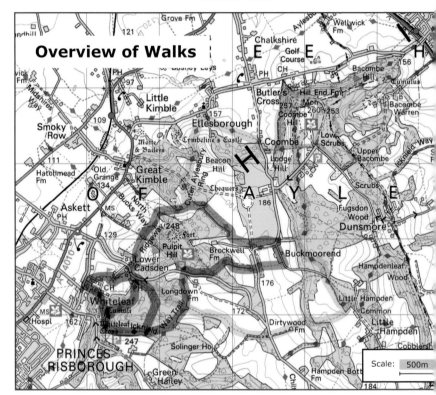

	Circular Walks	Distance	Ascent	Allow
	Short	**1¾ miles**	**110m**	**1½ hrs**
		2.8km	360ft	
	Medium	**4¾ miles**	**120m**	**3 hrs**
		7.6km	390ft	
	Longer	**7½ miles**	**220m**	**3½ hrs**
		12km	720ft	
	Figure of eight walks			
	Short + Medium	**6½ miles**	**230m**	**4½ hrs**
		10.4km	750ft	
Walk Choices	Short + Longer	**9¼ miles**	**330m**	**5 hrs**
		14.8km	1080ft	
	Medium + Longer	**12¼ miles**	**340m**	**6½ hrs**
		19.6km	1110ft	

Special Interests	S	M	L	Local (Miles)
Outstanding viewpoints	✓	✓	✓	
Beech woodland	✓	✓	✓	
Coombe Hill Monument re Second Boer War (overlooking the Vale of Aylesbury)			✓	
Whiteleaf Cross (large cross of chalk overlooking The Vale of Aylesbury from Whiteleaf Hill)	✓	✓		
Chequers - The country house of the Prime Minister of the United Kingdom		✓	✓	
Next nearest pub: Red Lion Whiteleaf HP27 0LL 01844 344476				3
Nearest Town:				
Wendover				5

Checkpoint grid references for GPS /Geocaching (Treasure Hunting)

Medium	
1	SP 826 045
2	830 054
3	835 055
4	841 050
5	847 046
6	837 045
7	834 044
8	829 037
9	822 038

Short	
1	SP 826 045
2	820 044
3	823 037
4	827 040

Longer			
1	SP 826 045	8	848 059
2	833 042	9	849 067
3	843 037	10	845 063
4	848 038	11	837 066
5	857 041	12	834 059
6	854 045	13	834 054
7	849 050	14	827 050

Looking over Chequers

LOWER CADSDEN SHORT WALK

1¾ miles (2.8km) • Ascent 110m (360 ft) • Allow 1½ hours

Quite a tough starter walk going across a golf course and then to the top of Whiteleaf Hill above the Whiteleaf Cross, before coming back down-hill through a beautiful beech wood.

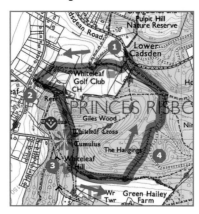

Checkpoints:

1 From the car park of the Plough, walk 30m **past** the pub, and **turn left** onto a footpath. **Go ahead** ascending to the right, with nice views to the right, before descending to the left to **go around** a thatch-roofed house. On arriving at the Golf Course ('Whiteleaf Golf Club'), **turn left** to go **slightly left of straight across** the fairway aiming for a gap in the hedge opposite. Once through the gate to come off the golf course, turn **half left** to cross the field in front of the cricket pavilion to a metalled drive and **turn right**. After 50m, **turn left** on a footpath between houses to arrive at a drive. **Proceed ahead** on the drive for 50m and then **turn left** uphill on a bridleway.

2 **Go straight ahead steeply uphill** for 250m (ignoring a right turn after 100m) to a major track/ footpath crossing. **Turn half right** onto a marked bridleway to **ascend** quite steeply through woodland. As you approach the top of the hill, **go through a gate** and **proceed ahead** to first level out and then arrive at another gate. You will go through this second gate shortly, but first of all pause to turn right and go over to a wooden barrier from where you have a wonderful panoramic view. Below the barrier lies the 'Whiteleaf Cross'. Return to the gate and now pass through it onto a wide track. *Note: The information board re the Neolithic Barrow is on your right.* **Continue ahead** on this wide, level, track for 200m to then **turn left** off the track onto a bridleway.

3 You are now walking along the top edge of 'The Hangings' wood. A beautiful beech wood. **Keep ahead**, more or less on the level, for nearly 400m (¼ mile), to then **turn left** on a permissive path and **descend** quite sharply through the woodland *(check the map to see the route of this permissive path.)*.

④ Keep ahead on this path bearing slightly left at the valley floor before **turning left** onto a wide path (joining from your right) to arrive back at your starting point.

Rural scene

Coombe Hill and monument

From Coombe Hill towards Ellesborough

LOWER CADSDEN MEDIUM WALK

4¾ miles (7.6km) • Ascent 120m (390ft) • Allow 3 hours

A very pleasant walk with a close up of Chequers; even passing through its grounds! Also tranquil walking through beech woods and an outstanding viewpoint at Whiteleaf Hill.

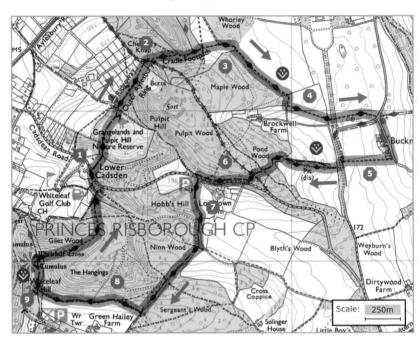

Checkpoints:

1 From the car park of the Plough, **go past** the pub, **turn left** along the main road which you cross almost immediately to enter woodland on a footpath. After approximately 200m, **go through a gate** and **bear half left. Keep ahead** on a wide grassy bridleway through 'Pulpit Hill Nature Reserve' then **cross** a bridleway passing through two gates. You are now on 'The Ridgeway'. There are good views to your left, now, as you pass the 'Butts' (an old army rifle range, on your right) to go up some steps to a cross-path. **Turn right,** staying on the Ridgeway, **through a gate on the left** after 20m and **bearing right** (still on the Ridgeway).

2 **Continue ahead** for 400m (¼ mile), winding downhill for a while before levelling out on the 'Cradle Footpath' and **ascending straight ahead** to enter a field through a gate. **Turn half right** (still on the Ridgeway) and cross the 200m or so of field to come to the perimeter fence of 'Chequers'.

3 **Bear right along the perimeter fence,** with a good view of 'Chequers' to your left. **Continue ahead** along the fence for 600m with very good views across the valley, when the path **turns left** through a gate.

4 You now **proceed across the property** of 'Chequers' for 400m

(¼ mile), keeping strictly to the footpath which crosses a metalled drive, to arrive at a bend on a road. **Cross the road** onto a metalled side-road to your right heading for 'Buckmoorend'. After 250m, having passed farm buildings **turn right** onto a footpath just beyond a house.

⑤ **Go straight ahead** across a field (350m), with wide views all round, to a road. **Cross the road** onto a wide track (bridleway) to **continue ahead** between fields to enter a thin strip of woodland ('Pond Wood'). **Keep ahead** on the path going steadily uphill, through Pond Wood. After a few hundred metres, the path levels out to come to a bridleway 'T' junction and **turn left.**

⑥ Almost immediately, **turn right** onto a path marked Riders Route which enters 'Pulpit Wood' and descends to the right. The path nears the road, when you **turn right** onto a bridleway (also marked as Icknield Way) for just 20m and **turn left.** Keep ahead on the Icknield Way parallel with the road (ignoring a left fork descending to the road) until you come to a 'T' junction track in front of a car park. **Turn left** on the track for just 20m to the road and **cross it** to continue on a bridleway (it is also,still, the Icknield Way)

⑦ **Go ahead** on the bridleway (Icknield Way) into 'Hobbs Hill'. **Continue ahead** through 'Ninn Wood' on the same bridleway, always going uphill for 1km, ignoring all turnings off. At one point on the way up, the bridleway bears half right for 20m before bearing left again and continuing uphill. As you reach the top of the hill and meet a junction of bridleways **turn right.**

⑧ **Keep on this bridleway,** which follows the top edge of the wood (with a field to the left of it) for nearly 800m (½ mile). First it goes slightly downhill, before bearing left and then continues ahead on the level to arrive at a footpath 'T' junction where you **turn right.**

⑨ You have now re-joined the Ridgeway path. After 200m, you arrive at Whiteleaf Hill. If you stand at the wooden barrier, you are above the Whiteleaf Cross and have a wonderful panoramic view before you. Once satiated, **turn round** (so you are backing onto the barrier) and head **straight across** to the woodland and **descend** on the Ridgeway footpath through 'Giles Wood' back to your start point.

LOWER CADSDEN LONGER WALK

7½ miles (12km) • Ascent 220m (720ft) • Allow 3½ hours

There are no fewer than six outstanding viewpoints on this walk, not least at Coombe Hill monument. Quite a tough, but very varied, walk.

Checkpoints:

① From the front door of the Plough, **turn right** and follow a track that runs along the left hand side of the car park. After 300m **fork left** at a prominent path interchange and then, 200m further on, **turn right** onto a path heading immediately uphill. After 100m **turn left** onto a narrow footpath (waymarked Purple Route) that heads steeply, windingly, uphill. The path levels out and **continues ahead** through 'Ninn Wood' until it meets a bridleway.

② **Continue across the bridleway** to **go ahead** on the footpath. Coming out of the wood, with fine views to your left, **continue ahead** along the right hand edge of three fields for 1km to arrive at a metalled drive.

3 **Turn left** onto the drive to come out onto a road. **Cross the road** onto a footpath heading towards Hampden Chase (marked as 'Dirtywood Farm' on the map at the time of going to press). Approaching the property, **turn left** around it on a permissive path. Between here and entering 'Hengrove Wood' there are good views, as you ascend, looking to your left towards Chequers.

4 On entering the wood, **continue ascending** for 50m before **bearing half right** to follow yellow arrows on the trees ahead. **Continue up** through 'Hengrove Wood', with a footpath joining from the left as the path levels out, to come out of the wood after 200m, into a field. With the wood on your right, continue to **ascend** for 150m, before going through a gap in the hedge and continuing for a further 200m on the right hand side of the hedge to enter a wood.

5 100m into the wood, you come to a 'T' junction of paths and **turn sharp left,** joining the Icknield Way. After 100m, **turn right** out of the wood and **continue ahead** on the level, with the wood on your right, for 400m (¼ mile) to come out of the field onto a major cross path junction.

6 **Proceed ahead** on the path signed (all of!) Bridleway, South Bucks Way and Icknield Way. The path descends gradually to the left through 'Chisley Wood' for 650m to arrive at a major cross-track junction. **Turn right** onto the Ridgeway.

7 **Go uphill** on the Ridgeway for approximately 200m through 'Goodmerhill Wood' and then **turn left** as the path levels out. Stay on the 'Ridgeway', more or less straight on through the wood, on the level, following the arrows on the trees, to arrive at a road after 800m (½ mile) and turn right.

8 **Go up the hill** on the road for approximately 100m, before **turning left off it,** again keeping to the Ridgeway path. After 250m, come out of the wood through a gate and **turn left** downhill for 50m. Then **turn right** along the top of the hill (still on the Ridgeway), with fantastic views to your left, including that of Chequers. Just over 400m (¼ mile) on, more or less on the level and with fantastic views to your left all the way, you arrive at the Coombe Hill Monument, with its panoramic views.

9 With your back to the Boer War plaque on the monument, go **slightly left** of **straight ahead** to sharply descend away from the monument. It is a *very, very* steep descent, so please take it carefully! Ignore two cross paths, to **turn sharp left** at the bottom of the hill and **proceed ahead** for 800m (½ mile) and more or less on the level, with the golf course immediately on your right.

10 **Turn right** at a cross path (at the end of the golf course) and in 100m come to a road at 'Coombe Hill Farm'. **Cross the road, turn right** and walk along the roadside footpath for 100m before **turning left** to cross an 800m (½ mile) long field.

11 From the field **turn right** on to a track for 125m to meet a road at Ellesborough. **Turn left** onto the footpath opposite the church and, almost immediately, **turn left** into a field. Ascend the field, **go through a gate** and then bear **half right** to go round the base of 'Beacon Hill' (with good views to the right). **Descend into and ascend via steps from** 'Ellesborough Warren' to enter a field, with good views to your right.

12 **Cross the field** into 'Whorley Wood'. **Cross a drive** and as you

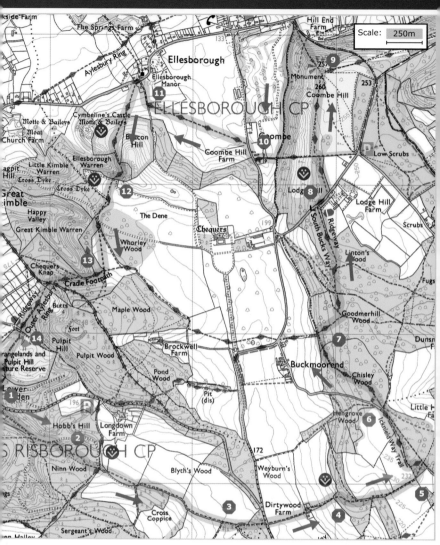

come into a field ahead, **turn right on entry.** After **descending** slightly, then **rising again** and bearing left at the top of the hillock, you have very good views to your right. **Turn left** along the hillock's flat top to arrive at a path 'T' junction. **Turn right** onto 'The Cradle Footpath' (re-joining the Ridgeway).

13 **Keep ahead,** more or less on the level, for 350m, to **cross a by-way,** then **go down some steps** into a field (with lovely views to the right). **Proceed ahead** across the field, passing the disused rifle range, and keeping to the left hand edge for 400m (¼ mile) when you arrive at cross-paths.

14 **Cross straight over,** entering 'Grangelands and Pulpit Hill Nature Reserve' *Note: A notice board here gives information on Grangelands and the Rifle Range.* **Proceed straight downhill, forking right** and keeping on the 'Ridgeway' to go through a small wood and arrive at 'Cadsden Road'. **Turn left** onto the road to come back to the starting point.

Start point: The Full Moon, Hawridge Common, Cholesbury, Bucks HP5 2UH 01494 758959 Customer parking at pub
Non-customer parking: nearby roadside

There are a great variety of landscapes at Cholesbury to give clear choices of walks. If you wish not to be too energetic, then take the short or medium walk as half day walks, or combine them for a whole day. The longer walk is a lot tougher, but excellent!

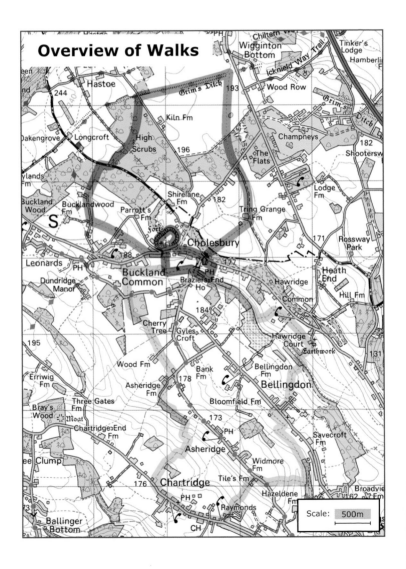

Special Interests	S	M	L	Local (Miles)
Outstanding viewpoints	✓		✓	
Beech woodland	✓	✓	✓	
Windmill Disused tower mill	✓	✓	✓	
Cholesbury Camp Iron Age hill fort	✓	✓	✓	
Grim's Ditch Pre-historic ditch earthworks		✓		
St Mary's Church Hawridge			✓	
Next nearest pub: The Blue Ball Asheridge HP5 2UX 01494 758305				1½
Nearest Town:				
Berkhamsted				4

Checkpoint grid references for GPS /Geocaching (Treasure Hunting)

Medium
①	SP 935 070
②	928 072
③	920 074
④	926 091
⑤	939 094
⑥	939 082
⑦	942 075
⑧	936 072

Longer
①	SP 935 070	⑨	937 036
②	941 064	⑩	928 041
③	945 063	⑪	933 046
④	948 056	⑫	929 053
⑤	946 050	⑬	931 055
⑥	946 046	⑭	927 063
⑦	949 040	⑮	924 065
⑧	943 041	⑯	925 067

Short
①	SP 935 070
②	934 068
③	928 072

	Circular Walks	Distance	Ascent	Allow
	Short	**1¾ miles**	**10m**	**¾ hr**
		2.8km	30ft	
	Medium	**4¾ miles**	**Negligible**	**2 hrs**
		7.6km		
	Longer	**8¼ miles**	**160m**	**4 hrs**
		13.2km	525ft	
	Figure of eight walks			
	Short + Medium	**6½ miles**	**10m**	**2¾ hrs**
		10.4km	30ft	
	Short + Longer	**10 miles**	**170m**	**4¾ hrs**
		16km	555ft	
	Medium + Longer	**13 miles**	**160m**	**6 hrs**
		20.8km	525ft	

Walk Choices (vertical label)

CHOLESBURY SHORT WALK

1¾ miles (2.8km) • Ascent 10m (30ft) • Allow ¾ hour

A gentle walk which includes passing the windmill and going round the embankment of the Iron Age fort.

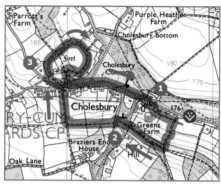

Checkpoints:

1 From the start position (as if coming out of the Full Moon car park) **turn right** and then **immediately right** again (over a stile) to see the windmill behind the pub. **Turn left** for 30m to then **turn right** behind a hedge for 25m. Then **turn left** over a stile to **go ahead** along the top of the field, **over another stile** and reach the far top corner of the field. Here, **turn right** down the hill onto the valley floor, where you **turn right.** After about 200m, look up to your right and see the windmill. You pass some neglected greenhouses and sheds and arrive on a driveway, leading to a road.

2 **Turn left** on the road and then, almost immediately, **right** onto a footpath and into a field. **Proceed ahead** for 300m over several stiles before arriving at a double kissing gate and **turn right,** ascending with the fence on your right and coming out on the road close to the fort. **Turn left** on the road and then take the **right hand fork** into Parrott's Lane. After 75m, **turn right** on the drive that leads to the church, which also leads to the fort (Cholesbury Camp). Go through the gate on the drive and then, almost immediately, **turn left** into the fort area.

3 **Go ahead** along the left embankment, ignoring all left hand turns, eventually walking along the bottom of the ditch. **Bear right** upwards to the top of the right embankment as directed by a white arrow on a tree. **Go over** a stile to exit the wooded area, **turn left** and **cross another stile.** Keep to the left hand side, passing an old storage building before **turning left** through a gate and going along a wide track back to the road and **turning left** back to the start point.

Beechwood scene

The windmill at Cholesbury

Rural scene

CHOLESBURY MEDIUM WALK

4¾ miles (7.6 km) • Ascent negligible • Allow 2 hours

A tranquil walk through beech woods and across open fields, passing the windmill, fort, and Grim's Ditch; negligible change of height.

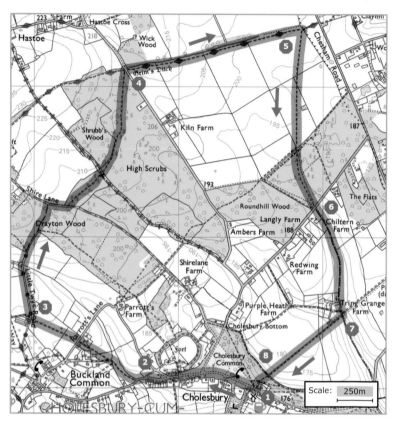

Checkpoints:

1 From the start position (as if coming out of the Full Moon car park) cross over to the common and **turn left** along it, passing the cricket square, cricket pavilion, the village hall and the fort (Cholesbury Camp) You are looking for a footpath 200m beyond the junction with 'Parrott's Lane' at the bottom of the hill, on the **right hand side** of the road.

2 **Enter** a field and **keep right** at the fork in the centre of the field. **Continue ahead** through two more fields, crossing 'Parrott's Lane' and another field and **turn right** onto 'Little Twye Road'.

3 Continue past 'Beechwood Farm' on a bridleway which goes **directly through** 'Drayton Wood' to 'Shire Lane'. **Turn right** and, after 125m **turn left** onto a footpath to go straight through 'Shrubs Wood', crossing a bridleway and then a track to reach a road.

4 **Cross** this road and proceed on the Chiltern Way (and 'Grim's Ditch'). This next kilometre is a lovely walk through typical beech woods and brings you to a kissing gate which you **DON'T** go through.

5 Instead, turn **sharp right** leaving the Chiltern Way and walk across the level field to 'Roundhill Wood'. On entering the wood, ignore left and right paths and head **half right** across the wood following white arrows on trees and yellow topped guideposts.

6 Coming out on a road, **cross it** and follow the bridleway passing 'Chiltern Farm' to 'Tring Grange Farm' where you **have to be careful not to take the wrong path.**

7 Take the **second footpath on the right,** ignoring the first one and then, a few metres past High Croft House (not named on your map) go through a kissing gate, to **proceed ahead** with the hedge on your right. The contour lines are quite close, meaning that you are climbing uphill quite sharply and, after it levels out, you can see the top of the Windmill ahead of you that sits behind the Full Moon pub, your destination.

8 The path then descends to a valley floor, which **you cross,** and rises up the other side to the right of a prominent tree, onto Cholesbury Common opposite the Full Moon, with the Windmill behind it.

CHOLESBURY LONGER WALK

8¼ miles (13.2km) • Ascent 160m (525ft) • Allow 4 hours

A lovely walk with outstanding views on the way, passing the windmill, St Mary's Church and a variety of fields and woods.

Checkpoints:

1 From the start position (as if coming out of the Full Moon car park) **turn right** and then **immediately right** again (over a stile) to see the windmill behind the pub. **Turn left** for 30m to then **turn** right behind a hedge for 25m. Then **turn left** over a stile **to go ahead** along the top of the field, **over another stile** and reach the far top corner of the field. Here **turn right** down the hill onto the valley floor where you **turn left. Go straight on** through a strip of woodland, ignoring the crossing path, before emerging from the wood into an open field with some woodland on your right.

2 Continue **straight ahead** to a hedge at the far end of the field, cross over the stile, **turn left** and go sharply uphill (with the hedge on your left hand side) Look back across the valley for some fine views.

3 At the top of the hill, the path levels out for 100m to reach a crossing path. Don't cross the stile, rather **turn right** in front of it and walk, with the fence on your left, towards 'Hawridge Place'. Pass 'Hawridge Place' to its left, crossing its drive as you continue ahead. Cross a muddy track ('Hawridge Lane') and a field to pass 'Hawridge Court'. Looking left, as you pass the house, you can see behind it St Mary's church. Then, 100m on, there is a gate in your path and, to its right, a hedge with trees in it. When you reach the gate, **do not go through it.** Rather, **turn sharp right** in front of it and descend, with the hedge and trees **on your left,** through another gate and continue down to the valley floor again.

4 **Turn left** and after 75m, **turn right** through a kissing gate to climb steeply uphill. Towards the top, **bear half left** towards a prominent house in the top left hand corner of the field. You come out of the field with 'Hilltop Farm' on your left, on a sharp corner of a residential road. **Turn right** along it to come out at 'Bellingdon' on to the main road.

5 **Cross** the road, **turn right** and then, almost immediately, **turn left** onto a footpath. After 75m, **turn left** through a gate and keep to the left hand edge of the field. Good views here to the right. Arriving at a track, **turn right** onto it and **go ahead onto a footpath** after 50m. This path comes out onto a wide field where you **turn left** and enjoy wonderful panoramic views.

6 Keeping to the top edge of the field, **proceed ahead.** After 800m (½ mile) of magnificent views, **turn right** just before 'Captain's Wood'.

7 **Descend** following the left hand hedge of the field before **climbing quite steeply** (half way up, the path goes through a gap in the hedge) to a road. **Turn right** on the road and then **left** onto a footpath just past 'Tile's Farm'.

8 This path **descends sharply** and then **rises again** (passing Chartridge Park caravan site) to a drive. Turn **half right** up the drive to a road. **Turn right** and walk through Chartridge.

9 There is a good roadside footpath nearly all the next kilometre to 'Lime Tree Farm' (your target). The roadside footpath ends about 200m before your destination, when you have to **cross the road** to face oncoming traffic to arrive at your turning.

10 At the farm **turn right** onto a bridleway. There are lovely views as the bridleway descends, turning sharp right, before turning left and **going left** around the bottom edge of the field.

11 After 200m on the level, **turn right** still on the bridleway, and ascend towards 'Braid Wood'. The bridleway then follows its right hand edge. As the hill begins to level out and you are close to the end of the wood, look out for some large wooden huts on your left. Here **turn left** off the bridleway passing between the huts. *Note: Take care not to miss the footpath, the sign may be slightly obscured.*

12 **Go straight ahead** through Braid Wood and as you come out of it, ignore the footpath to your right, but a few metres further on **turn right** onto the bridleway ahead.

13 Pass through 'Asheridge Farm' onto a metalled track and 20m before reaching the road, **turn left** onto a footpath.

14 The footpath goes past 'Wood Farm' and continues ahead (ignoring the crossing bridleway) bearing half left through a strip of woodland. **Turn right** along the outside edge of the woodland to come out onto 'Oak Lane'.

15 **Turn left** on Oak Lane, then almost immediately **turn right** onto a footpath going across the field to the far left corner.

16 In that corner **turn right** on a crossing path and keep ahead, with the hedge on your left, through several fields until you come to a road. **Turn left** here which takes you uphill and back to your starting point.

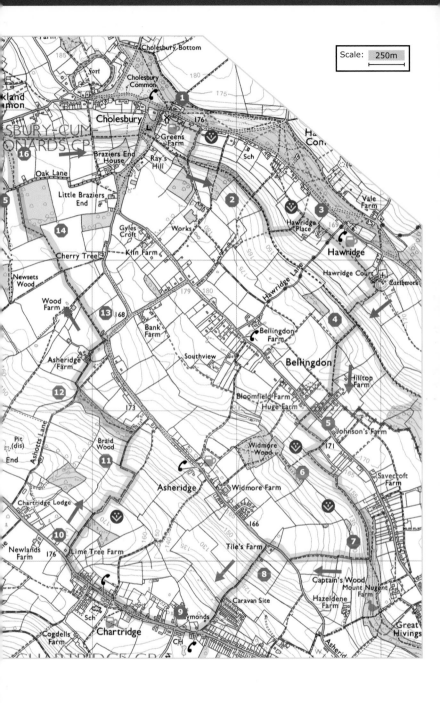

Scale: 250m

9. Ashridge

Start point: Ashridge Monument, Moneybury Hill, Berkhamsted HP4 1LX **Car park on site**.
Café on site: Brownlow Café 01442 851670

Ashridge monument and the Ashridge Estate attract many, many visitors. There is a marvellous café there open from early until late and ample parking. It also has some wonderful walking choices to suit everyone. The longer walk here links the monument to another prominent hill and landmark in the Chilterns- Ivinghoe Beacon.

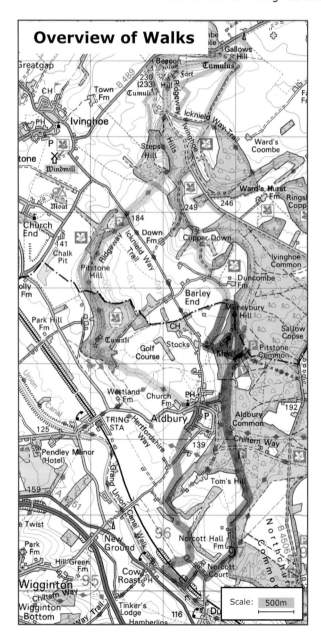

Special Interests	S	M	L	Local (Miles)
Outstanding viewpoints	✓	✓	✓	
Beech woodland	✓	✓	✓	
Bridgewater Monument - built in 1832 in memory of 3rd Duke of Bridgewater	✓	✓	✓	
Aldbury Stocks		✓	✓	
Ivinghoe Beacon Prominent hill and landmark			✓	
Next nearest pub: The Greyhound Inn, Aldbury HP23 5RT 01442 851228				2½
Nearest Town:				
Tring				5

Checkpoint grid references for GPS /Geocaching (Treasure Hunting)

Medium

1	SP 971 132
2	969 118
3	927 112
4	970 105
5	963 102
6	960 112
7	962 116
8	966 124

Longer

1	SP 971 132	8	962 160
2	968 137	9	954 148
3	964 147	10	950 140
4	964 155	11	953 131
5	966 163	12	958 127
6	970 168	13	966 124
7	961 167		

Short

1	SP 971 132
2	968 137
3	966 133

	Circular Walks	Distance	Ascent	Allow
	Short	**1¼ miles**	**75m**	**1 hr**
		2km	245ft	
	Medium	**4¾ miles**	**130m**	**2½ hrs**
		7.6km	425ft	
Walk Choices	Longer	**7¾ miles**	**220m**	**4 hrs**
		12.4km	720ft	
	Figure of eight walks			
	Short + Medium	**6 miles**	**205m**	**3½ hrs**
		9.6km	670ft	
	Short + Longer	**9 miles**	**295m**	**5 hrs**
		14.4km	965ft	
	Medium + Longer	**12½ miles**	**450m**	**6½ hrs**
		20km	1145ft	

ASHRIDGE SHORT WALK

1¼ miles (2km) • Ascent 75m (245ft) • Allow 1 hour

Although this is a short walk (just 1¼ miles) there is a very steep hill towards the end of it and if you aren't as fit as you'd like to be, you may need to simply turn round and return the way you came. For those fit enough, an excellent starter walk!

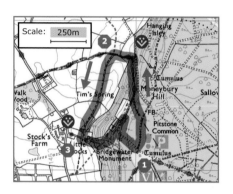

Checkpoints:

1 From the car park head for the Ashridge Bridgewater Monument then turn right to **enter woodland** on the mobility track. After 150m, **fork left** onto a footpath, heading downhill. After 200m, the path joins a bridleway (coming from the left) to continue downhill. It takes a sharp left turn to come out of the woodland, with lovely views to the right and comes shortly to a cross-path.

2 **Turn left** at the cross-path into a field. **Keep ahead** on the right hand side, running parallel with the wood on your left and continue ahead into the next field where there are lovely views to your right. **Pass** a house on your right and come to a drive ('Little Stocks') on which you **turn left.**

3 **Go up** the drive and **straight ahead** onto a footpath to the right of a house. **Enter woodland** to **ascend** very steeply. *Note: This hill is particularly tough and strenuous and should you have any doubts about your fitness, simply back track the way you came.* Pause on the ascent, not just for breath, but to look out for a house further up the hill to your left. When you come closer to it, you are looking at the back of the house and you have to get round to the front of it. **Continue ahead** at a waymarked cross path (the house is then above you to the left) and 20m *(only!)* further on **fork left** (on a narrow, rather overgrown unmarked path) to go around the house to a bridleway 'T' junction. **Turn left** for 50m along the bridleway to reach Rangers Cottage, then **turn right** along the wide track for 200m to arrive back at the Monument and the start point.

Bluebell wood at Ashridge

Pitstone windmill with Ivinghoe Beacon

View from Ivinghoe Beacon

ASHRIDGE MEDIUM WALK

4¾ miles (7.6km) • Ascent 130m (425ft) • Allow 2½ hours

The first couple of miles on this walk are more or less on the level through woodland, before descending to cross several fields with wonderful views to your left. In Aldbury you can see the stocks by the pond in the middle of the village, before heading back up (very steeply!) to the starting point

Checkpoints:

1 From the car park at the Ashridge Bridgewater Monument, **go past** the café and **bear left** onto a wide track entering woodland. **Keep right** at a possible fork just after entry, descending at first, then as the path levels out **ignore** a prominent downhill footpath to your right. After 800m (½ mile) you reach a track 'T' junction, **turn right** to descend for 20m before turning **sharp left** back into the wood. **Continue ahead**, crossing a drive diagonally, then after 250m **cross a road** at 'Gryme's Dell' (where there's a car park to your left).

2 **Continue ahead** for 800m (½ mile), ignoring left and right turns, to arrive at a waymark with five direction symbols. **Fork Right** onto a bridleway.

3 **Continue ahead** on the bridleway, with a field on your right, for 400m (¼ mile) to arrive at a track and **turn left** on it. **Proceed ahead** for 400m (¼ mile), passing several houses and 'Norcott Hall' on your right to arrive at an 'off road' car park before a bend in the road.

4 **Keep ahead on the road** going quite sharply downhill to **turn right** at the next road junction. **Proceed ahead** on the road, on the level, for 125m and then **turn left,** descending slightly for 200m, and just before reaching a railway bridge **turn right** off the road onto a bridleway.

5 Walk alongside the railway line for 250m before turning right on the path and proceed a further 200m **straight on** to come to 'Norcott Court Farm'. **Go ahead** on a footpath to the right of the farm buildings and immediately head **half left** across a field with fine views to your left. **Follow this path through** another field (with fine panoramic views).

6 **Ascend** through a third field, with fine views front and to your left, before entering a fourth field. **Beware:** coming into this field **keep right,** following the edge of the wood at 'The Hangings'. Then **turn half left** to cross down the field, **turning right** onto a road ('Newground Road').

7 **Proceed ahead** on the road for just 150m and **turn left** onto a footpath. **Proceed ahead** 75m and **turn right** through a metal gate to cross a field (hedge on your left) and enter a cul de sac. **Continue ahead,** along the road that passes The Valiant Trooper pub on your right, to come to a 'T' junction and **turn right,** in front of the pond and stocks, onto Tom's Hill Road.

8 After 50m **turn left** off the road onto a footpath (Signposted to Ashridge Visitor Centre/ Café) that heads steeply uphill for 800m (½ mile) directly back to the starting point

ASHRIDGE LONGER WALK

7¾ miles (12.4 km) • Ascent 220m (720ft) • Allow 4 hours

An outstanding walk, partly linked with the outstanding viewpoints you constantly meet. You have outstanding views after descending from the woods to cross several fields at the beginning, and outstanding views both heading towards and returning from Ivinghoe Beacon.

Checkpoints:

1 From the car park head for the Ashridge Bridgewater Monument then turn right to **enter woodland** on the mobility track. After 150m, **fork left** onto a footpath, heading downhill. After 200m, the path joins a bridleway (coming from the left) to continue downhill. It takes a sharp left turn to come out of the woodland, with lovely views to the left and right. **Ignore a wide track** to the right as you enter open space and arrive immediately at a cross path.

2 **Turn right (90 degrees)** at the cross-path. *Note: the sign may be difficult to see in the undergrowth, but you can see the path's continuation to the left.* Go straight ahead across the field, through a gap in the hedge and then half left across the next field to **turn left** on a metalled track. After 125m along the track, **turn right** onto a footpath which ascends gradually for just 75m. **Ignore** the first footpath sign to your left, and **continue ahead** a few metres then go through a gate and turn **sharp left** to continue climbing to the right. There are very good panoramic views to the left, and looking back. After 400m (¼ mile) **turn left** onto a wide track coming in from your right.

3 **Keep ahead** on this track, with 'Crawley Wood' to the right, as it undulates for nearly a kilometre to a road, where you **turn left.**

4 **After 50 metres, cross the road** and go ahead down a wide track through a gate marked Access Land. There are fantastic panoramic views here, including the 'White Lion' of Whipsnade and the Dunstable Downs. Keep to the track as it bears gradually left through 'The Coombe' for 800 metres (½ mile) to the **bottom left** hand corner of the field.

5 **Turn sharp right** into the next field and go ahead on a footpath for 800m (½ mile) before **turning left** at the end of it.

6 For the next kilometre, **proceed straight ahead** uphill for 75m, before going through a gate and continuing up the hill for a further 150m. Then bear left whilst still gaining height to walk along the ridge (with lovely views left and right). You then arrive at Ivinghoe Beacon (on 'Beacon Hill'), from where you have wonderful panoramic views.

7 **T**urn **90 degrees left** to descend on an extremely wide, and well-worn, track to arrive on the corner of a road. **Cross the road** to join a footpath (the Ridgeway) **bearing up to your right.** After 50m, **fork right** onto a footpath (still the Ridgeway, marked with an acorn symbol, that you are going to follow for the next 3km (2 miles). After the fork, proceed uphill for 100m before descending to go through a gate and **turn left.**

8 **Go uphill,** keeping to the left hand edge of the field **to go through** a wood as the path levels. Coming out of the wood and going across the top of 'Steps Hill' there are very good panoramic views to your right. The path sweeps to the right, round the top of a deep valley, descending to a road.

9 **Go straight** over the road, walk through a car park (car park symbol on map) to **continue ahead** on the Ridgeway footpath. **Ascend gradually** (you can go left of the mound in front of you) for 800m (½ mile) to the top of 'Pitstone Hill', with fantastic panoramic views to front and right. Here there is a marker post directing you to **fork right** to stay on the Ridgeway path.

10 **Immediately,** you begin gently descending, again with great views to the front and right, for 250m to enter a wood in front of you ('Aldbury Nowers'). **Keep ahead** on the Ridgeway foot path for a further 800m (½ mile) through the wood to arrive at a 'T' junction of paths. *Note :This is where you leave the Ridgeway!!!* **Turn left** to **come off** the Ridgeway path.

11 After 30m ascending, **turn right** and **continue ahead** through the wood - you will see the golf course through the trees to your left. After 150m come out of the wood onto the 'Stocks Golf Club' course at a signposted cross- path. Descend **straight ahead,** following the left hand hedge **to go through** a gap. **Proceed ahead** on the same line, straight across the golf course, following markers, to come off the course at a cross-path.

12 **Continue ahead** over the cross-path. Then **cross** three fields to come out onto a road ('Station Road') and **turn left,** on the road, past the church. Shortly you arrive at cross roads, with the stocks to your left, and continue ahead onto Tom's Hill Road.

13 **Proceed ahead** for 50m and **turn left** onto a footpath that winds sharply uphill for 800m (½ mile) to bring you back to the starting point.

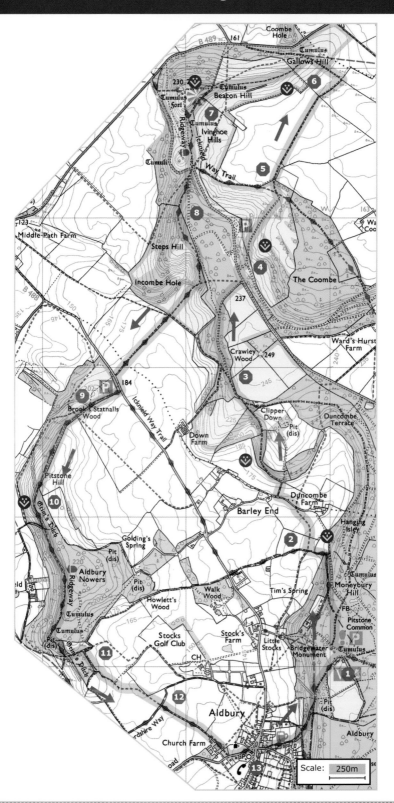

10. Little Gaddesden

Start point: The Bridgewater Arms, Little Gaddesden, Berkhamsted HP4 1PD 01442 842408 Customer parking at the pub.
Non-customer parking: on Church Road, alongside the outdoor bowling club (within 500 yards of the Bridgewater Arms)

This is a wonderful location for walking. To walk along Golden Valley at any time of the year is tranquil, but in Autumn with the golden leaves of the beech trees serenading you, it is magical. But this location brings you much more……….

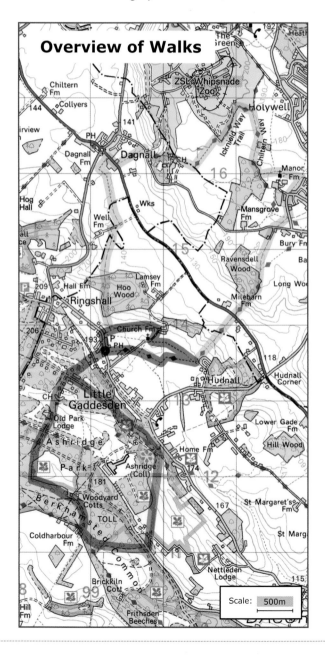

Special Interests	S	M	L	Local (Miles)
Outstanding viewpoints	✓	✓	✓	
Beech woodland	✓	✓	✓	
Golden Valley		✓		
Ashridge House Now a business school		✓		
Whipsnade Zoo			✓	
Next nearest pub: The Red Lion Dagnall HP4 1QZ 01442 843020				2
Nearest Town:				
Hemel Hempstead				7

Checkpoint grid references for GPS /Geocaching (Treasure Hunting)

Medium	
❶	SP 992 136
❷	994 130
❸	999 123
❹	999 115
❺	998 111
❻	991 111
❼	987 116
❽	983 120
❾	984 126
❿	986 134

Longer			
❶	SP 992 136	❽	TL 013 168
❷	SP 996 136	❾	TL 007 164
❸	TL 004 135	❿	SP 998 163
❹	TL 010 142	⓫	SP 994 162
❺	TL 014 147	⓬	SP 993 156
❻	TL 018 154	⓭	SP 993 153
❼	TL 013 163	⓮	SP 993 147

Short	
❶	SP 992 136
❷	SP 999 139
❸	TL 004 135
❹	SP 996 136

	Circular Walks	Distance	Ascent	Allow
Walk Choices	Short	**2 miles**	**Negligible**	**1 hr**
		3.2km		
	Medium	**4¾ miles**	**70m**	**2 hrs**
		7.6km	230ft	
	Longer	**7 miles**	**135m**	**3½ hrs**
		11.2km	425ft	
	Figure of eight walks			
	Short + Medium	**6¾ miles**	**70m**	**3 hrs**
		10.8km	230ft	
	Short + Longer	**9 miles**	**135m**	**4½ hrs**
		14.4km	425ft	
	Medium + Longer	**11¾ miles**	**205m**	**5½ hrs**
		18.8km	655ft	

LITTLE GADDESDEN SHORT WALK

2 miles (3.2 km) • Ascent negligible • Allow 1 hour

A very easy 'starter' walk across fields, on the level, with two outstanding viewpoints on the way.

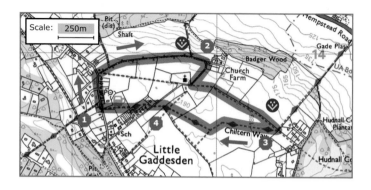

Checkpoints:

1 Facing the Bridgwater Arms, **turn left** along the pavement for 200m, past the shop, to **turn right** onto a restricted byway. **Proceed ahead** (ignoring right and left turns) for 75m on a wide track to enter a field ahead, through a gate. **Keep ahead** close to the hedge on your left hand side, crossing two fields to arrive at Church Farm, after 800m (½ mile). There are excellent views here to your left.

2 **Turn right** onto a metalled road in front of the farm and **proceed ahead** with the church in view to the right. After 200m, as the road bends right (around the church) **turn sharp left** onto a footpath taking you across a field into another. In the second field, keep to the left hand edge for 400m (¼ mile) to the far corner of the field. **Pause here** to look through a large gap to your left for a wonderful panoramic view.

3 **Do not come out of this field.** Rather, **turn sharp right** onto the 'Chiltern Way' footpath which passes to the right of an oak tree, not more than 30m away from where you're standing. **Proceed ahead** on the path for 800m (½ mile) keeping on the Chiltern Way as you cross into another field to arrive at a metalled road in front of a house (looking right here, you have a clear view of the church).

4 **Turn left** on the metalled road for a few metres before coming off it by **turning right** and continue to follow the Chiltern Way back to Little Gaddesden and the start point.

Golden Valley

Between Dagnall and Little Gaddesden

View from beyond the church

LITTLE GADDESDEN MEDIUM WALK

4¾ miles (7.6km) • Ascent 70m (230ft) • Allow 2 hours

A lovely walk along Golden Valley, with a view of Ashridge House to your right, through beech woodlands and across Ashridge golf course; includes two outstanding viewpoints.

Checkpoints:

1 **Go out of the back of the car park** of the Bridgewater Arms onto a footpath that **crosses** a track and continues downhill. At the end of the gardens **turn left** onto the Ashridge Boundary Trail and proceed for about 800m (½ mile) on the level, through a woodland to a metalled road.

2 **Turn right** on to the road for a few metres before coming off it onto a footpath on the left (running beside the road), that **bears left** into the beautiful 'Golden Valley'. **Proceed ahead** along the valley floor for 800m (½ mile) before **crossing** a wide track coming from the left.

3 After 50m, **leave** the Ashridge Boundary Trail, by **bearing half right** up the slope of the valley. In 150m, in the middle of a dip, go through a gate and continue ascending on the path aiming for the top right hand corner of the field. **Rise steadily** for 400m (¼ mile), with fine views ahead and to your left.

4 As the path levels out, **pass through** a gate on to a narrow path. **Continue ahead,** on the level and with fine views until you **descend** on a metalled drive to a road.

5 **Cross** the road and join a bridleway rising **to the right.** After a short stretch of woodland it comes out onto grassland and runs along the **right hand edge** of the field, rising gradually for nearly 800m (½ mile).

6 At the end of the field, it bears right, entering the woodland, and after 200m is joined by another bridleway, coming from the left, to arrive at 'Coldharbour Farm'. **Turn right** onto a wide bridleway through woodland for 400m (¼ mile) to a crossing track 50m before 'Woodyard Cottages'.

7 Turn left at the crossing track and **proceed ahead** on the bridleway with Woodyard Cottages on your right. **Continue ahead** for 400m (¼ mile) to enter woodland and, almost immediately, **turn right** (90 degrees) onto the Chiltern Way footpath.

8 Continue ahead for 250m, just inside the wood (field to your right). **BEWARE!** You come to a fork off to the right, with a prominent path (The Foresters Walk) following that fence. **Do not take that fork to the right!** The Chiltern Way (on which you must stay) **goes straight ahead** into the woodland. After another 250m, you arrive at a track.

9 Cross straight over the track to **proceed ahead** on a metalled road (still on the Chiltern Way) for 400m (¼ mile) **passing** the 'Prince's Riding', a golf fairway and the front of 'Old Park Lodge'. Just beyond the lodge, come off the road onto a footpath, **continuing ahead** through woodland. After 150m, you come out onto a fairway, and head half left **between** the Ashridge Golf Club House and the practice putting green. **Pass** the club house **to the left,** heading uphill to the right of the fairway, on a footpath that takes you through a short strip of trees to the left of the Golf Club car park. **Turn left** onto the metalled drive to arrive at a 'T' junction of roads.

10 Cross straight over the road onto a footpath (the Chiltern Way), and proceed ahead between high fences to **cross** a fairway and **descend** through a short stretch of trees. The path (still on the Chiltern Way) then ascends between gardens and crosses a track back to the start point.

LITTLE GADDESDEN LONGER WALK

7 Miles (11.2km) • Ascent 135m (425ft) • Allow 3½ hours

A lovely walk across fields, through beech woodlands, around Whipsnade Zoo's perimeter fence, and across the Whipsnade Golf Club's course; walks can't come much better than this one...

Checkpoints:

1 Facing the Bridgwater Arms, **turn right** along the pavement for 30m and **turn left** onto the Chiltern Way. After 400m (¼ mile) you arrive at a metalled road.

2 Cross the road and bearing half left (still on the Chiltern Way) cross two meadows and then go diagonally left across a very lengthy field (800m, ½ mile) to the top right hand corner where there are cross paths.

3 Continue half left on the Chiltern Way into the next field, with a hedge on your right, with lovely panoramic views. Half way down the hill, the footpath joins a bridleway coming in from the right and they continue together (with the hedge still on your right) down to a main road ('Hemel Hempstead Road').

4 **Cross the road** and **continue ahead** ascending quite steeply, with a hedge on your left. Approximately ¾ of the way up, go through a gap in the hedge and continue rising with the hedge now on your right. You then go along the edge of 'Ravensdell Wood'.

5 As you come out of the wood, on the level, **continue ahead** on the bridleway. *Note: you leave the Chiltern Way here, as it turns off to the right, 50m beyond the wood.* **Stay on** the bridleway for nearly 400m (¼ mile) to **cross** 'Common Road' and descend **half right,** for 200m, to the far right hand corner of a field and **turn left** onto a road (Valley Road).

6 **The road ascends** for 300m to a junction with Church Road. Keep round the bend to the right on Valley Road and about 15m after the bend **turn left** onto a footpath.. Arriving at a cross path after 250m, **turn left** along the edge of the field. **Pass** the Studham church on your left to **continue ahead** across a track into a field. After 200m, **enter** a wood and immediately **turn right** at a cross path. You have now joined the Chiltern Way again, and come out of the wood after just 200m and continue on the Chiltern Way.

7 **Proceed ahead,** for nearly 800m (½ mile), with a hedge on your right and extensive views to your left across a wide, open field. As you come to the end of the field and enter woodland, **turn immediately left** (to leave the Chiltern Way and now join the Icknield Way)

8 After 50m, the perimeter fence of Whipsnade Zoo appears on your right. **Continue ahead** for nearly 800m (½ mile), first bearing left, then (near the end) bearing right, before emerging onto 'Whipsnade Park Golf Club' course.

9 **Proceed straight ahead,** to the left of an oak tree, and **continue on that line** (with confirmation waymark posts following the 'Icknield Way') across a number of fairways for 400m (¼ mile), until you come to the last fairway. At this point, you come to a 'T' junction of paths, and **turn right** still following the Icknield Way, along the middle of an avenue of trees. As you come to the end of the avenue of trees, you need to aim (following the directions on an Icknield Way sign) for the golf tee to the right of the Golf Club House. Behind the tee is an entrance to woodland and the continuation of the Icknield Way.

10 **Descend sharply** through woodland, pausing half way down to admire the views ahead and to the right. At the foot of the hill, **turn right** onto 'Studham Lane'. After 100m, **turn left** onto a narrow footpath (still the Icknield Way) that descends for 400m (¼ mile) to the A4146 Main Road and **turn right.**

11 **Go along the pavement** for 150m, passing Dagnall School, and the entrance to 'Cross Keys Farm' before **turning left** onto a footpath that goes around the outside of the farm. After rounding the farm buildings you arrive at a track that comes from the back entrance of the farm and turn right on it. There are good all-round views as the path ascends **half right** across the field. *Note: if you look to your right, there is a long row of hedge/ trees and you are aiming for the left hand end of them.* When you reach this point, you enter the next field.

12 Go straight across the next field and then continue ahead with a hedge on your right. At the end of the hedge, turn sharp right to follow a bridleway sign onto a drive rising towards 'Well Farm'.

13 Turn left off the drive onto a footpath/ bridleway after 125m. You are now on quite a wide track that bears round to the right, with a large hedge to your right. This wide track stops abruptly at the end of the hedge but a narrow path continues across a field for 150m to enter another field. Cross the next field to enter 'Hoo Wood'.

14 On entering, ascend quite steeply straight ahead and continue on that line right through the wood. Coming out of the wood cross a field for 150m to a 'T' junction track and turn right. Arriving after 75m at a main road, turn left to come back to the starting point.

Further walk choices for the experienced map reader

You will need to have one or more of OS EXPLORER maps 171, 172, 181, 182 to follow/mark-up routes; I mark up my routes with pencilled arrows.

There are **14 locations** (numbered 11-24 continuing on from the other section of the guide) **each with 3 walk choices** (two half- day, and one whole day) between **3 -13** miles.

Walk choices location map

Numbers 1-10 = Fully described routes at locations linked to map extracts:

1. Hambleden; 2. Pishill ; 3. Turville; 4. Piddington;
5. Stokenchurch; 6. Great Kingshill; 7.Lower Cadsden; 8. Cholesbury;
9. Ashridge; 10. Little Gaddesden
(see Table of Contents of all these locations on page 5)

Numbers 11-24 = For experienced map readers with OS EXPLORER maps
(see Table of Contents opposite)

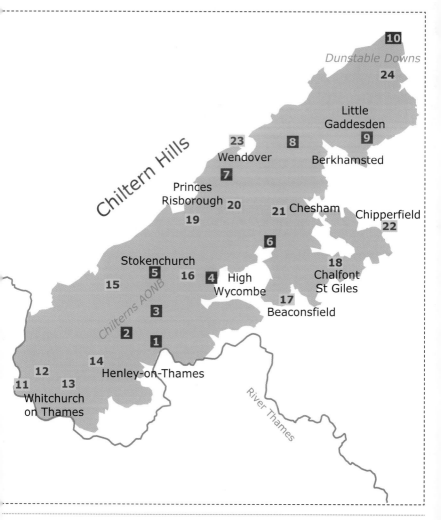

Starting point: The Sun, Hill Bottom, Whitchurch Hill, Reading, RG8 7PU
tel 0118 984 2260
Non-customer parking roadside.

Nearest town: Whitchurch-on-Thames 2 miles.
The Sun is marked on your map at grid reference 645 793

The Sun, Whitchurch Hill

Half day medium (4¾ miles)

Special interest: Panoramic view over Thames Valley; tranquillity

1. Turn right out of Sun car park and shortly (within 50m) turn left onto a footpath going South between houses through a cul de sac. At the road, turn right and then left to continue south (to left of 'Whitchurch Hill')
2. Turn left along the 'Chiltern Way' and turn right on the bridleway past 'Pathhill Farm'.
3. Pass 'Hardwick House' and turn left onto the 'Chiltern Way' just past 'East Lodge'
4. Stay on 'Chiltern Way' through 'Bottom Wood' and turning left at 'Collins End'.
5. Come off 'Chiltern Way' to return to starting point via the right of 'Whitchurch Hill'.

Half day longer (7¼ miles)

Special Interests: Hartstock Nature Reserve; Panoramic views over Thames Valley; tranquillity

1. Turn right out of Sun car park, cross main Whitchurch/ Woodcote road and turn left (to right of 'Coombe End Farm')
2. Pass 'Beech Farm' and 'Stoneycroft Plantation'
3. Before 'Whitchurch-on-Thames' turn right onto the 'Thames Path' (passing 'Avoca Farm')
4. Pass 'Coombe Park Farm' and 'Lower Hartsock Wood' to turn right at 'Hattonhill Shaw'.
5. Pass 'Upper Gatehampton Farm', 'Great Chalk Wood' and 'Bottom Farm' to arrive at a road below 'Blackbird's Bottom'.
6. Cross over road to continue on path crossing 'Eastfield Lane' before turning right in 'Little Oaken Wood' and right again to pass 'Great Oaks' back to the starting point.

Whole day walk (combined medium and longer walks) 12 miles

Starting point:
The Cherry Tree Inn, Stoke Row Rd, Henley-on-Thames RG9 5QA 01491 680430 Non-customer parking roadside.
Nearest town: Henley 4 miles.

The Cherry Tree Inn grid reference 683 840

The Cherry Tree Inn, Stoke Row

Half day medium (3½ miles)

Special interest: Tranquil beech woodland; fine views; tranquillity

1. Turn left out of the Cherry Tree Inn and left again to turn right onto a bridleway on entering 'Bush Wood'.
2. Keeping to the bridleway go through 'Bear Wood' to turn right through 'Burnt Platt' passing 'Barn Farm'.
3. Continue ahead to turn right passing 'Wyfold Court' and 'Neal's Farm'.
4. Turn left at 'Busgrove Wood' and turn right on 'Busgrove Lane' back into Stoke Row.

Half day longer (8½ miles)

Special Interests: Panoramic views; Maharaja's Well, beech woodlands; tranquillity

1. Turn right out of the Cherry Tree Inn and left by the church (beyond the 'Maharaja's Well').
2. Take the footpath that goes 'Dogmore End', 'Scots Farm','Garsons Farm'.
3. Go via 'Warren's Chase', turn right and left to 'Wellplace Farm' and then turn right to 'Handsmooth Farm'.
4. Just beyond, turn left through 'Fludger's Wood' and passing 'Homer Farm' to arrive at 'Kit's Lane'.
5. Cross the lane to go to 'English Farm', 'Barley Hill'; and to 'Upper Shaw'.
6. Pass 'Howberrywood' to turn right at 'Highmoor Farm'.
7. Return to starting point via 'Bush Wood'

Whole day walk (combined medium and longer walks) 12 miles.

Starting point:
The Maltsters Arms, Rotherfield Greys, Henley-on-Thames RG9 4QD
tel: 01491 628400
Non-customer parking in front of church.
Nearest town: Henley 2 miles.

Maltsters Arms grid reference 725 824

The Maltsters Arms, Rotherfield Greys

Half day medium (3½ miles)

Special interest: Greys church; fine views; tranquillity

1. From the pub, go past the church and along the road to go (half right) across to 'Cowfields Farm', then head South towards 'Upper House Farm'.
2. Turn right at 'King's Farm' and again right at the corner of 'Crosscroft Wood' to go below 'Bottom Barn' to 'Arundel'.
3. Take the path to the left of 'Crowsley Park Woods' to turn left at 'Crosslanes'.
4. Then take the footpath on the right back to the starting point.

Half day longer (7½ miles)

Special Interests: Greys church; Water Tank at Bix; Greys Court; Bix Manor; panoramic views; tranquillity

1. Take the path opposite to the church that goes to the right of 'Pindars Wood' and then go North to then follow the path which zig-zags to the left of 'New Farm'; continue North.
2. On entering the wood, turn right before shortly turning left to come out to the right of 'Lambridge Hill'.
3. Go to the right of the church and cross the roads to turn right up 'Great Hill'.
4. Turn left on the 'Oxfordshire Way' to stay on it into 'Middle Assendon'.
5. Turn right then left onto the footpath to Bix church.
6. Cross the road and go past 'Bix Manor Farm' and take the path that goes past 'Lawrence Farm'.
7. Join the 'Chiltern Way' passing to the left of 'Park Cottage' and in front of 'Greys Court'.
8. Turn left on the road to join the path at 'Greys Green' towards 'Pindars Wood'. Turn right on the footpath through 'Pindars Wood' back to the starting point.

Whole day walk (combined medium and longer walks) 11 miles

14. Middle Assendon (OS Explorer map 171)

Starting point:
The Rainbow Inn Middle Assendon Henley-on-Thames RG9 6AU
tel: 01491 574879
Park in long lay-by close to pub.
Nearest town:
Henley-on-Thames 1 mile

The Rainbow Inn grid reference: 739 857

The Rainbow Inn, Middle Assendon

Half day medium (3½ miles)

Special interest: Fantastic panoramic view; tranquillity

1. Cross the road and join the 'Oxfordshire Way' to go below 'Crockmore Farm' and then head in the direction of 'Henley-on-Thames', still on the 'Oxfordshire Way'.
2. Turn off right after 'Great Hill' and 'Henley Park' to arrive at 'Lower Assendon'.
3. Cross B480 to walk up 'Bix Hill' (narrow lane) to 'Bix'.
4. Return to 'Middle Assendon' via the common and the footpath half way down 'White Lane'.

Half day longer (7½ miles)

Special Interests: Lovely views; tranquillity

1. Take footpath up to 'White Lane' and on to Bix church.
2. Cross A4130, pass 'Bix Manor Farm' to turn right at 'Brawn's House'.
3. Pass 'Lawrence Farm' and turn right on entering 'Famous Copse'.
4. Turn right onto the 'Chiltern Way' and follow it through 'Bix', 'Bix Common' and 'Bix Bottom'.
5. Continue through 'Freedom Wood' to 'Lodge Farm' and turn right through 'Park Wood'.
6. Cross the road at 'Stonor' into 'Almshill Wood' and go around to 'Coxlease Farm'
7. Head South to 'Paradise Wood' and back to 'Middle Assendon'.

Whole day walk (combined medium and longer walks) 11 miles.

Starting point:
The Fox & Hounds, Christmas Common, Watlington OX49 5HL tel 01491 612599
Non-customer parking nearby, roadside.

Nearest town:
Watlington 1½ miles.

Christmas Common grid reference 714 932

The Fox & Hounds, Christmas Common

Half day medium (3¾ miles)

Special interest: Panoramic views; beautiful beech wood; tranquillity

1. Turn left out of the pub, go past 'Hill Road' to turn left onto the 'Oxfordshire Way'.
2. Turn left onto 'Swan's Way' and then turn left onto a permissive path **(Note: this permissive path is not marked on the map)** that goes from the right of 'White Mark Farm' to join the 'Watlington Hill' footpath **(coming down from the car park below 'Watlington Hall Farm')**. Turn right on joining that path.
3. In 250m turn left to go towards 'Watlington Park'.
4. Ignore another path (on the left) to 'Lower Dean' and continue through 'Lower Deans Wood' to come out on the road next to the starting point.

Half day longer (7½ miles)

Special Interests: Fantastic panoramic views; World War II Bomber memorial; tranquillity

1. Turn left out of the pub and at the end of the road cross onto a path to the right of 'Christmas Common'.
2. This path goes down below 'Shotridge Wood' and 'Barnfield Hanging Wood' to join the 'Chiltern Way' coming from 'Northend' and continuing East.
3. Just before the 'Chiltern Way' sign, turn left to pass 'Commonhill Wood' and go through 'Bowley's Wood' to 'Wellground Farm'.
4. Turn left to enter 'Langleygreen Plantation'. Turn left at a crosspath to 'Lower Vicar's Farm'.
5. Continue ahead, to enter 'Cowleaze Wood', come to a road and turn left to 'Field House'.
6. Cross the road to join a path through 'Shirburn Wood' to turn left on the 'Oxfordshire Way 'at 'Pyrton Hill House' to return to the starting point.

Whole day walk (combined medium and longer walks) 11¼ miles.

Starting point:
Chris's Café, Wycombe
Road, Studley Green,
HP14 3XB
Non-customers parking
in side road nearby (Old
Oxford Road).
Nearest towns:
Stokenchurch 2 miles;
High Wycombe 3 miles

Chris's Cafe grid
reference: 791 951

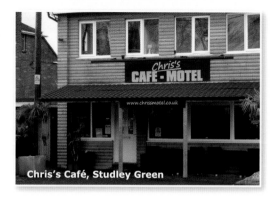

Chris's Café, Studley Green

Half day medium (3¼ miles)

Special interest: Fantastic panoramic views; beech woodlands.

1. Cross the road to go through 'Thirds Wood' and 'Fillingdon Wood'
    heading South to 'Barn Wood'.
2. Turn right into 'Barn Wood' and then turn right again into
    'Leygrove's Wood'.
3. Continue ahead to 'Bigmore Farm' and take the footpath running
    beside 'Gibbon's Farm'.
4. Continue down on the road to 'Horsley's Green'.
5. Turn right onto the bridleway just before the A40 to come back to
    the start position.

Half day longer (7 miles)

Special Interests: Lovely views; beech woodlands.

1. Cross the road to turn right on entering 'Thirds Wood' and then
    left past 'Wycliffe Centre'.
2. Pass 'Dell's Farm' and then bear right in 'Leygrove's Wood' to head
    straight for the underpass of the M40 at 'Cadmore End' (to the
    left of 'Kensham Farm').
3. Go through 'Hanger Wood', branching right in the middle to come
    out close to 'Gravesend'.
4. Turn left on the road into 'Fingest', passing 'Manor Farm' and
    taking the next left path towards 'Hanger Farm'.
5. Above the farm bear right, then left towards 'Rackley's Farm'.
6. Re-cross the motorway ('Kensham Farm' to your left) and go
    through 'Cadmore End Common' to 'Huckenden Farm'.
7. Head North, taking the paths that lead down to the left of
    'Fillingdon Farm' and come back to the starting point ('Studley
    Green') via 'Thirds Wood'.

Whole day walk (combined medium and longer walks) 10¼ miles.

Starting point:
The Royal Standard of England, Forty Green, Beaconsfield HP9 1XS
01494 673382
Parking next to the pub.

Nearest town:
Beaconsfield 1½ miles.

Forty Green grid reference: 923 919

The Royal Standard of England, Forty Green

Half day medium (4 miles)

Special interest: the pub itself: claims to be oldest pub in England; lovely views; tranquillity

1. Turn left out of the pub and turn right on a path that takes you to 'Lude Farm'.
2. Turn right then left and then left again to go above 'Sniggs Wood' to 'Wycombe Heights Golf centre'.
3. Turn right (leaving the 'Chiltern Way') to pass the Golf Club House ('CH').
4. Pass 'Town Farm' and 'Pond Wood' to join a road until the right of 'Beacon Hill'.
5. Turn right, go through 'Gatemoor Wood' and keep on the path ahead until it joins the road just a few hundred metres from the start point.

Half day longer (7½ miles)

Special Interests: Wild Flower Meadow; beech woodland; tranquillity

1. Turn right out of the pub and turn left on the footpath that passes 'Longfield Wood' to then turn right at 'Coppice Hoop', following the 'Chiltern Way' path.
2. Turn right to go past 'Fords', crosses the road and continues through 'Twichells Wood' to 'Penn Bottom'.
3. Fork right in 'Branches Wood' to 'Glory Farm' and then via 'Lowlands' and 'Hertfordshire House' and below 'Luckings Farm'.
4. Go South then to 'Wood Cottage' before turning right to head through 'Great Beard's Wood' and 'Netherlands Wood' to 'Knotty Green'.
5. Continue to cross the road towards 'Forty Green'.
6. After approx. 400 m, turn right onto a footpath that runs behind the houses back to the starting point.

Whole day walk (combined medium and longer walks) 11½ miles.

18. Chalfont St. Giles (OS Explorer map 172)

Starting point:
The Ivy House, London Road, Chalfont St Giles HP8 4RS tel: 01494 872184
No non-customer parking.
Nearest towns:
Chalfont St Giles 1 mile; Amersham 2 miles.

The Ivy House grid reference: 983 957

The Ivy House, Chalfont St Giles

Half day medium (3½ miles)

Special interest: Beech woodland; golf course (Harewood Down House); tranquillity

1. Turn left out of the Ivy House car park and take the path next to the Ivy House that goes across the golf course.
2. Bear left to go via 'Coke's Farm' below' Little Chalfont', past 'Works' to above 'Cemetery'.
3. Turn left to head South and turn left on A413 'London Road East'.
4. After 300metres, turn right to cross the 'River Misbourne' and turn left onto the 'South Bucks Way'.
5. Turn left on the road (Farm Lane) at 'Lower Bottom House Farm' back to the start point.

Half day longer (7½ miles)

Special Interests: Lovely viewpoints; beech woodland; golf course (Oakland Park); tranquillity

1. Turn left out of the Ivy House car park and take the path next to Ivy House that goes across the golf course. Opposite the Club House, turn right and follow the edge of 'Pollards Wood'.
2. After crossing the A413 turn left on the 'South Bucks Way', before immediately turning right onto the 'Chiltern Way' to pass 'Hill Farm House' and 'Works' to walk briefly along the edge of 'Hodgemoor Woods'.
3. Turn left to pass through 'Chalfont St Giles' and go across 'Oakland Park Golf Club' and past 'Greyhound Training Track'.
4. Cross 'Narcot Lane' and zigzag through, passing 'Windmill Farm' to turn left onto the 'South Bucks Way'.
5. Keep on the 'South Bucks Way' through Chalfont St Giles and turn right on 'Farm Lane' at 'Lower Bottom House Farm' to return to starting point.

Whole day walk (combined medium and longer walks) 11 miles.

19. Bledlow (OS Explorer maps 181 and 171)

Starting point:
The Lions of Bledlow,
Church End, Bledlow HP27
9PE tel: 01844 343345
Non-customer parking
roadside.
Nearest town:
Princes Risborough
1½ miles

The Lions of Bledlow grid
reference: 776 021

The Lions of Bledlow, Bledlow

Half day medium (5¼ miles) map 181

Special interest: Lovely views; tranquillity

1. Turn left out of the pub and go behind it on the path that has 'The Warren' to the left of it.
2. Cross 'Wigan's Lane' and go through 'Tumuli' passing 'Lodge Hill' on the 'Ridgeway'.
3. Go through 'Princes Risborough Golf Club', cross the railway line, then turn left on the 'Chiltern Way'.
4. Keep on the 'Chiltern Way' back to 'Bledlow'- via 'Frogmore Farm' and 'Bledlow Homes'(where you turn left along the road in front of the church)

Half day longer (7½ miles) maps 181 and 171

Special Interests: Lovely views; beech woodlands; Radnage church, tranquillity

1. Start on map 181. Turn left out of the pub and go behind it onto the path 'Midshires Way'.
2. Go through 'Hempton Wainhill' up to the car park on 'Chinnor Hill'.
3. Map 171. Go through the car park and continue on the road and take the footpath below 'Woodlands Farm' that re-joins the road on a bend.
4. Turn right on the road for 100m to take the path on your left at '242'
5. Follow this path as it joins 'Bledlow Circular Ride' to 'Town End'.
6. Turn left across a field and then turn left on the road below Radnage church ('Radnage Lane').
7. You are now on the 'Chiltern Way' which you follow back into Bledlow via 'Neighbour's Wood', 'Callow Down Farm', crossing 'Wigan's Lane', and continuing on the footpath ending up opposite 'Church End'.

Whole day walk (combined medium and longer walks) 12¾ miles.

20. Parslow Hillock (OS Explorer maps 181 & 172)

Starting point:
Pink and Lily, Pink Road,
Princes Risborough HP27
0RJ tel: 01494 489857
No non-customer parking.

Nearest town:
Princes Risborough
1½ miles

The Pink and Lily grid
reference: 827 019

The Pink & Lily, Parslow Hillock

Half day medium (3¾ miles) 181 OS Map

Special interest: Hampden House; beech woodlands; tranquillity

1. From car park, go around the pub and go down towards 'Lily Bank Farm'.
2. Go via 'Coppice House' and 'Keepershill Wood' towards 'Ferns Farm'.
3. Turn right on the road and then turn left onto the footpath that goes through 'Great Hampden' to turn left at 'Hampden House'.
4. Go through 'Barnes Grove' on the 'Chiltern Way'.
5. Turn right at 'Redland End' and then left at the cross-path to return to 'Parslow Hillock' and the starting point.

Half day longer (7¼ miles) 181 & 172 OS Maps

Special Interests: Lovely viewpoints; beech woodlands; windmill at Loosley Row; tranquillity

1. Map 181 From car park, go around the pub and go down towards 'Lily Bank Farm'.
2. Enter woodland to your left and then turn right along the edge of 'Monkton Wood' via 'College Plantation' to map 172. Immediately turn right onto a footpath next to 'Speen'.
3. Cross the road and join the footpath above 'Pye Corner'.
4. Go via 'Guys Spring' to 'Works' (at 'Walters Ash') and turn right onto the main road.
5. After 1km turn left onto the footpath through 'Park Wood', turning right in the middle of the wood to go to 'Bradenham Wood'. Turn right on 'Smalldean Lane' and then left onto path past 'Grymsdyke Farm' and turn to map 181.
6. Follow the path back to the main road and turn left on it towards 'Loosley Row'.
7. Turn right onto the 'Chiltern Way' back to 'Lily Bank Farm' and turn left back to starting point.

Whole day walk (combined medium and longer walks) 11 miles.

Starting point:
The Black Horse,
Mobwell, Aylesbury Rd,
Gt.Missenden HP16 9AX
tel: 01494 862537
Non-customer parking
roadside.
Nearest town:
Gt. Missenden ½ mile

The Black Horse grid
reference: 891 020

The Black Horse, Mobwell

Half day medium (4 miles)

Special interest: Great views; beech woodland; tranquillity

1. Cross road from pub and take path to 'Rignall Farm'; go through 'Rignall Wood' and turn left on the road after passing 'Pankridge Farm'.
2. Cross A4128 to turn left on path 200m down the opposite road.
3. Continue ahead on that path through 'Angling Spring Wood' to go under the railway line. Turn right **ahead of the High Street**, at a 'T' junction of minor roads that brings you onto the high street after 250m.
4. Turn right in front of the school for 200m and turn left on 'South Bucks Way' through 'Abbey Park' and keep on the 'South Bucks Way' back to 'Mobwell' and the Black Horse.

Half day longer (7 miles)

Special Interests: Lovely views; beech woodlands; tranquillity

1. Facing the Black Horse, go around towards its car park and turn right across the fields.
2. Cross the A413 and head up to 'Park Farm'. Turn left, then right, through 'Springfield Farm' to 'Lee Common' and then turn left at 'Lee Clump' towards 'Lee Gate'.
3. Take footpath below 'Kingsgate Farm' to join the 'Chiltern Way' past 'Durham Farm', crossing the A413, and through 'Cockshoots Wood'.
4. Turn left at 'Cobblershill Farm' to join the 'South Bucks Way' down to starting point.

Whole day walk (combined medium and longer walks) 11 miles

Starting point:
The Windmill, The Common, Chipperfield, WD4 9BU
tel: 01923 264310
Parking opposite/close to the pub.

Nearest town:
Hemel Hempstead 4 miles.

The Windmill grid reference: 040 014

The Windmill, Chipperfield

Half day medium (3½ miles) OS Map 182

Special interest: Beech woodland; varied landscape; tranquillity

1. When facing the pub, turn left along the road. After 250m, below 'Rose Farm', turn left going southwards and then turn right on the track in front of 'Belsize Farm'.
2. Cross the road, passing the pub (The Plough) and join the road that goes towards 'Whitedell Farm'.
3. About half way along the road, turn left to 'Rose Hall Farm' and turn right onto the 'Chiltern Way' past 'Bragman's Farm' and 'Newhouse Farm'.
4. Turn right to go through 'Lower Plantation'.
5. Turn right onto 'Holly Hedges Lane' and follow the 'Hertfordshire Way' through 'Woodman's Wood' before zigzagging at 'Dunny Lane' back to the starting point.

Half day longer (8 miles) OS Maps 182 and 172

Special Interests: Lovely views; beech woodlands; tranquillity

1. Start on Map 182. There's a multi branch of footpaths coming out from the pub and the one you should set off on is the one marked 'Public Footpath'. Aim for the pond via 'Chipperfield Common' and 'Tumuli' to turn right through 'Hunterswood' to 'Commonwood'.
2. Fork left 250m past the pub and continue on map 172.
3. Turn left at 'Bottom Lane' and immediately right into 'Sarratt'.
4. Turn right, passing the pub (The Cricketers) and then left of 'PO' to go through 'Sandfield Wood'.
5. Turn left onto the 'Chiltern Way' and follow it, via 'Church End', to cross the Chess and take the footpath above 'Nicholas Spring'.
6. Pass 'Mountwood Farm' into 'Chenies'.
7. Cross the road. Proceed up the Chenies Manor drive. Turn right beyond the church to go around the Manor to arrive above 'Greathouse Farm'.
8. Take the footpath below 'Coney Wood' and turn right to cross the road towards 'Latimer'.
9. Turn right beyond the Chess to go through 'Church Rems of' to join the 'Chess Valley Walk' East, passing 'Mill Farm', then turning left at 'Valley Farm'.
10. Go through 'Hanging Lane Wood' onto map 182.
11. Return to starting point via 'Rose Hall Farm', the pub at 'Belsize' and the path above the telephone symbol.

Whole day walk (combined medium and longer walks) 11½ miles.

Starting point:
The Shoulder of Mutton,
20 Pound Street,
Wendover HP22 6EJ
01296 623223

Non-customer parking in
central car park.

Shoulder of Mutton grid
reference: 866 077

The Shoulder of Mutton, Wendover

Half day medium (4 miles)

Special interest: Great views across Aylesbury Plain and Chequers;
beech woodland; Boer War memorial; tranquillity

1. Turn right out of car park. Go over bridge and turn left onto a
   path.
2. Head to 'Coxgrove Wood' then bear right within the wood to go up
   towards 'Dunsmore'.
3. Turn right at the top to go through 'High Scrubs' then 'Low Scrubs'
   (via the car park) and across to the 'Monument' on 'Coombe Hill'.
4. Turn right at the monument to follow the 'Ridgeway' into
   Wendover.

Half day longer (7½ miles)

Special Interests: Lovely views; Golf club; beech woodlands; Go Ape;
Café in the Woods; tranquillity

1. Turn left out of the car park and go down through the town,
   turning left on the 'B4009'.
2. 250m on the right, join the 'Aylesbury Ring' along the disused
   canal.
3. Continue along the canal to come off at 'Wellonhead Bridge'.
4. Go across the bridge and join the 'Outer Aylesbury Ring' path
   to then go via 'Aston Hill' to the Café in the woods/ Go Ape/
   Children's play-ground of 'Wendover Woods'.
5. Continue on the 'Outer Aylesbury Ring' through 'Wendover Woods'
   to turn right on 'Hale Lane' to come back into 'Wendover' centre
   and the starting point.

Whole day walk (combined medium and longer walks)
11½ miles.

Starting point:
The Red Lion, 50 Church Rd, Studham, LU6 2QA
01582 872530
Non-customer parking on the common, opposite the war memorial.
Nearest town:
Markyate 3 miles.

The Red Lion is marked on your map at grid reference 022 158

The Red Lion, Studham

Half day medium (3¾ miles)

Special interest: Panoramic views; tranquillity

1. Turn left out of the Red Lion onto the 'Dunstable Rd', crossing it onto a footpath opposite 'Bell Farm'.
2. Turn left at 'Hill Farm' onto 'Byslips Rd' and then right onto the footpath at 'Long Grove'.
3. Go along 'Roe End Lane' and turn right at 'Hollybush Lodge'
4. Turn right at 'Kennels Lodge' and return to starting point via 'Beechwood Farm', 'Goose Hatch' and 'Studham Common'.

Half day longer (7¼ miles)

Special Interests: Panoramic views; Chilterns Gateway Centre; Dunstable Downs; Tree Cathedral; tranquillity

1. Turn right out of the Red Lion and turn right almost immediately onto a footpath and then again on the path to the right of 'Studham'.
2. Turn left, then right on/off 'Dunstable Road' and turn left along the footpath meeting 'Buckwood Lane'.
3. Go through 'Heath Wood' then through the church yard at 'Whipsnade' and cross the road to join the 'Chiltern Way' to the 'Chilterns Gateway Centre'.
4. Return on the 'Icknield Way Trail', to turn left to the 'Tree Cathedral'.
5. Cross the road to go down 'Studham Lane' to turn right just before meeting the 'Dunstable Road' and pass through 'Linney Head' to turn left at Studham church back to the starting point.

Whole day walk (combined medium and longer walks) 11 miles.

AUTHOR'S PAGE

I am a retired Publisher of books for Business and Accountancy Students who has been in love with the Chilterns since I first walked there at the age of 12. At that time, a friend and I took a train out to Wendover (in the heart of the Chilterns) and walked the 20 miles back home to Rickmansworth (West London). We passed the Boer War Memorial at Coombe Hill, with its wonderful viewpoint over the Aylesbury Plain and Chequers (the Prime Minister's country residence), the tranquil beech woodlands overlooking the Misbourne Valley on the way to Great Missenden and the gentle Chess Valley between Chesham and Rickmansworth. I have revisited all these places many, many times in the intervening years and their beauty hasn't faded. I have always lived in the area and for the last ten years I have designed, and led, walks in the heart of the Chilterns for the U3a (University of the Third Age).

The inspiration for this book came from my daughter in law. She said one Sunday as she admired the peace and quiet of the Chilterns 'Please bring us here every Sunday to explore this wonderful area.' She was, of course, contrasting her urban rush and bustle with the tranquillity that is the trade mark of the Chilterns.

So I'm hoping that you will enjoy that tranquillity, too, with the contents of my book to help you.